SPORTS EQUIPMENT
MANAGEMENT

The Jones and Bartlett Series in Health Sciences

SPORTS EQUIPMENT
MANAGEMENT

MARCIA L. WALKER

University of Northern Colorado

TODD L. SEIDLER

Wayne State University

Jones and Bartlett Publishers

Boston   London

Editorial, Sales, and Customer Service Offices
Jones and Bartlett Publishers
One Exeter Plaza
Boston, MA 02116

Jones and Bartlett Publishers International
P.O. Box 1498
London W6 7RS England

Library of Congress Cataloging-in-Publication Data
Walker, Marcia
 Sports equipment management / Marcia L. Walker & Todd L. Seidler.
  p. cm.
 Includes bibliographical references.
 ISBN 0-86720-281-5
 1. Sports--Equipment and supplies. 2. Physical education and training--Equipment and supplies. I. Seidler, Todd L. II. Title.
GV745.W35 1992
796'.028--dc20

92-13401
CIP

Production Editor: John Servideo
Editorial and Production Service: Karen Mason
Cover Design: David Kelley
Prepress, Printing and Binding: R. R. Donnelley and Sons

Credits for Photographs

 Edora Pool Ice Center: Figures 5–1, 5–6, 5–17, 5–22, 5–23, 5–28

 Greeley Recreation Center, Greeley, Colorado: Figures 0–2, 0–4, 1–9, 4–2, 5–7, 5–16, 5–18, 5–24

 St. Norbert College: Figures 5–12, 5–26

 Tulane University: Figures 1–1, 1–10, 1–11, 1–12, 1–13, 4–9, 5–10

 University of New Mexico: Figures 0–1, 4–1, 4–3(a), 4–5, 4–9, 5–5, 5–31, 5–29, 5–33, 5–34, 7–1

 University of Northern Colorado, Physical Education Department: Figures 4–3(b), 4–4, 4–6, 4–7, 4–11, 5–2, 5–8, 5–9, 5–11, 5–13, 5–14, 5–19, 5–20, 5–21, 5–25, 5–30, 5–32

 University of Southern Mississippi, Athletic Department: Figures 4–10, 5–3, 5–4, 5–15, 5–27

 Zeni's M & W Sporting Goods Company: Figures 1–2, 1–3, 1–4

Contents

Preface

Purpose

This book is a practical manual about sports equipment for individuals involved with sports as the athletic director, equipment manager, coach, physical education teacher, leisure/recreational activity director, fitness/health club manager, sports club director, or practitioner.

Definitions

For the purpose of this book we use the following definitions: *Facilities* are the buildings used for some activity (Figure 0–1); *equipment* includes useable, nondisposable items that are added to a facility and are expected to be used over a period of years. These may be either fixed (backboards—Figure 0–2, scoreboards—Figure 0–3) or portable (uniforms, bats, balls, bleachers—Figure 0–4); and *supplies* are disposable and frequently replaced articles (athletic tape, marking pens).

Figure 0–1 ■ One example of a sports facility, the Albuquerque Sports Stadium, is home to the Albuquerque Dukes minor league baseball team.

FIGURE 0–2 ■ Backboards and scoreboards are examples of fixed equipment.

FIGURE 0–3 ■ Bleachers are portable equipment, which can be moved to allow floor space for activities that need no room for spectators to sit.

Acknowledgments

The authors wish to express their gratitude and appreciation to the following persons for their time, resources, and encouragement throughout the writing of this book. Without their help it would have been impossible to gather all the materials needed for this text and to produce the quality contained herein. We are indebted to them for their efforts.

David Bounds, Athletic Equipment Manager, University of Southern Mississippi

Peter Farmer, Physical Education Chairman, Tulane University

Rudy Garcia, Athletic Equipment Manager, University of New Mexico

Jeff King, Facility Manager, Parks & Recreation, Edora Pool Ice Center, Fort Collins, Colorado

Mary Merritt, Physical Education Equipment Manager, University of Northern Colorado

Mike Miles, Superintendent of Recreation, City of Greeley, Colorado

Mike Schuch, Athletic Equipment Manager, University of Northern Colorado

Joe Zeni, M & W Sporting Goods Company, Albuquerque, New Mexico

Special appreciation goes to our friends and loved ones for putting up with us during this endeavor.

SPORTS EQUIPMENT
MANAGEMENT

Chapter One

INTRODUCTION

"Give us the tools, and we will finish the job"
(Winston Churchill, cited in Resick, 1979, p. 254)

INTRODUCTION

Sports equipment has been used throughout history. We present a selection of interesting and diverse uses of sports equipment to provide an understanding of the dramatic changes in the development of sports equipment.

We focus on two basic eras: sports equipment in early societies and sports equipment in modern times. For further details, consult the selected readings listed at the end of this chapter.

Sports Equipment in Early Societies

One of the oldest activities known to use some type of sports equipment is archery.

> Archaeological excavations proved its existence over at least 10,000 years ago. Stone arrowheads were found in the skeletons of prehistoric beasts killed by the earliest hunters. They were discovered embedded in the bones of extinct, giant bison, elk, and huge rhinoceroses of the pre-glacial era, which had been buried under the ice for many millennia (Brasch, 1970, p. 8).

In Spain and France, spectacular cave paintings render men hunting animals by bow and arrow. Later, references to the bow and arrow appear in Homer's *Odyssey,* in passages of the Bible, in the metaphysical system of Zen Buddhism, in Shakespeare's plays, and so on. Although the bow and arrow originated as a means of self-preservation, it was the end of the sixteenth century before "archery began to gain widespread recognition as a sport" (Bourquardez & Heilman, 1950, p. 1).

Other archaeological evidence portrays sports equipment from the Egyptian civilization (3000–1100 B.C.). Sports that abounded during this period include various ball games, juggling, a hoop game, stick fighting, knife throwing, swinging of weights, a kicking game, and many other games using equipment of various types.

The Mycenaean Greek civilization (some time after 1800 B.C.) represents another important era in the history of sports implements (Harris, 1973, p. 139). This age was well represented with athletic festivals and contests, including the Olympic Games. Examples of equipment used in some of the sports, as illustrated on preserved Greek pottery, are the discus, the javelin, different types of balls, and the hoop and stick.

The Etruscan civilization (800–100 B.C.) offers other examples of sports equipment in early societies. Some of the activities during this period were discus throwing, javelin throwing, chariot racing, hunting, fishing, *ascolia* (attempting to stand on a greasy goatskin vase), and the use of dice, balls, and tops (Zeigler, 1988).

Finally, the greatest change in equipment for any sport has occurred in football. Although there is no proof, some historians believe that some form of football has been played throughout the ages. An early British document records a gruesome practice in which "some races used their enemies' severed heads as footballs" (Brasch, 1970, p. 144).

Fortunately, footballs of more acceptable types also were used. The Pharaohs used balls (for a game similar to football) that were made of fine linen or soft leather and were filled with straw or reed. "Other similar balls of man's earliest civilizations, in which two hemispherically shaped skins were sewn together, were filled with earth, grain, plant fibres, corn husks, or even pieces of metal" (Brasch, 1970, p. 145).

Having explored some interesting and diverse sports equipment used by early societies, we will look at sports equipment in modern times.

Sports Equipment in Modern Times

It was not until the middle of the nineteenth century that baseball appeared in America. Many different types of baseballs were used until 1866 when "the first standardized baseball was manufactured" (Bourquardez & Heilman, 1950, p. 28).

Perhaps the most important change in the development of the baseball is that the rubber center was substituted with a cork center in 1910. The first regulation regarding bats, established in 1863, stated that "bats had to be round, made of wood, could not exceed two and one-half inches in diameter and had no restrictions as to length" (Bourquardez & Heilman, 1950, p. 32).

In depicting another example of sports equipment in modern times, we discover that American football players first wore full-length hose, heavy jerseys, noseguards, shinguards, and tightly laced canvas jackets (developed by a Princeton player named L. P. Smock in 1877). Helmets, of any type, were not required until 1935. Figures 1–1, 1–2, and 1–3 show three different stages of football helmets.

FIGURE 1–1 ■ The first leather football helmets were made in the early 1900s.

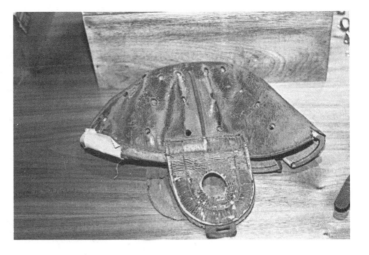

FIGURE 1–2 ■ In the late 1950s, Riddell made a football helmet with a plastic mouthguard.

FIGURE 1–3 ■ Football helmet and shoulder pads. These football shoulder pads were made of compressed paper by Rawlings in the 1940s.

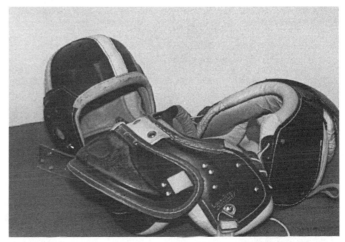

FIGURE 1–4 ■ Examples of 1990s football facemasks which are metal bar guards coated with rubber.

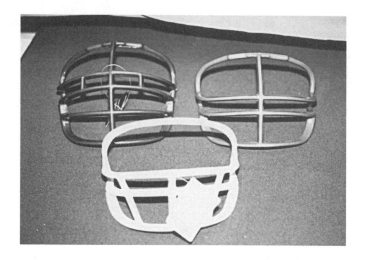

Other requirements for the sport soon followed: face protectors in 1960, chin-straps in 1973, National Operating Committee on Standards for Athletic Equipment (NOCSAE) certified helmets in 1980, and hip pads with tailbone protectors in 1984 ("And in the beginning," 1987). Figure 1–4 presents examples of contemporary facemasks.

Another sport that has shown considerable change in its equipment is basketball. Dr. James A. Naismith, who invented the sport in 1891, decided that "the ball should be large and light, easy to handle but difficult to conceal" (Brasch, 1970, p. 42). Therefore, the first ball used was a soccer ball.

A peach basket, suspended from the balcony, was used as the first basketball goal. A ladder was required to retrieve the ball from the basket. Eventually, the peach basket was replaced by a metal one and then by open loops fixed on poles or boards. Glass backboards were first introduced in 1909.

"The uniform consisted of knee-length padded pants or knee-length jersey tights with a quarter-length or sleeveless shirt." (Bourquardez & Heilman, 1950, p. 60). Another part of the uniform consisted of rubber suction-soled shoes that were developed for the game in 1903.

Other interesting examples of equipment used during the developmental stages of specific sports include: badminton–champagne corks stuck with feathers supposedly represented the first shuttlecock, in the modern version of the game (Pratt & Benagh, 1964); bowling—the first ball was made of stone, one-half spherical and the other half egg-shaped; boxing —the hands were protected by straps of soft leather wrapped around the knuckles and held in the fist; and golf—some believe it originated from Scottish shepherd boys knocking small stones into holes in the ground with a crook (Bourquardez & Heilman, 1950).

As has been shown, many different sports have emerged with tremendous changes made in the products which depict those sports. There have been changes in styles, types, and materials. Also, standards for most sports equipment have gradually been established as the sports themselves have evolved.

Finally, to gain a thorough understanding of the background of sports equipment, it should be noted that the Athletic Equipment Managers Association (AEMA) was formed in 1974. Prior to this time, no national organization had existed for equipment managers and there was no formal training available (Ferguson, 1990). Since that time, requirements for certification through the AEMA have already been developed and testing for certification is a current reality (Equipment Managers, 1990).

Although these examples represent a fraction of the history of sports equipment, it is evident that there have been enormous changes, not only in the physical materials, but also in the standards, and that these changes have had an impact on sports as we recognize them today.

DEMAND FOR CURRENT INFORMATION CONCERNING SPORTS EQUIPMENT

The original book on *Sports Equipment—Selection, Care, and Repair* (1950) was written by Virginia Bourquardez and Charles Heilman. Ten years later *Equipment and Supplies for Athletics, Physical Education, and Recreation* (1960) was published by The Athletic Institute and The American Association for Health, Physical Education, Recreation, and Dance (AAHPERD). Since that time, no major sports equipment texts have been published.

Obviously, the world of sports and sports equipment has undergone tremendous changes since 1960. Sports have flourished and sports equipment has become a multibillion dollar business. Sports administrators' responsibilities have expanded; new sports and sports industries have developed. Computerization is now a necessity. Monies awarded in lawsuits involving various aspects of sports products and equipment usage have grown to astronomical amounts. Innovative equipment has been developed. Even the administrative philosophy dealing with the acquisition, use, and maintenance of equipment is quite different than that which was in effect in the 1950s and 1960s.

THE ROLE OF EQUIPMENT IN SPORTS

The impact that sports has on our society and on the world is enormous. It exerts a powerful influence in several ways: sociologically, psychologically, politically, financially, and so on. Likewise, the amount and effect of the equipment that makes sports possible is virtually immeasurable.

Sociological Influences

George Bush keeps his 45-year-old Rawlings Claw in a drawer of his desk in the Oval Office. Oriole infielder René Gonzales keeps his gamer in a bag that once contained Wonder Bread. No other piece of sports equipment, perhaps no other inanimate object, exerts quite the hold on us that the baseball glove does. Most anyone who has played the game remembers a favorite glove from his or her youth, the one he or she hung from the handlebars of a bicycle (Wulf & Kaplan, 1990, May 7, p. 68).

How is sport sociological and what is the connection between sports equipment and society? Sport is sociological because "all sports involve humans interacting with other humans in a structured way" (Curry & Jiobu, 1984, p. 17).

In the United States, we are surrounded by sport. From a distance we see sport on television, in the movies, and in advertisements. As spectators, we watch our favorite teams compete, whether they are professional, collegiate, high school, club, or youth league. As participants, we are running, hitting, serving, throwing, spiking, sledding, riding, skating, hiking, or skiing.

It is difficult to imagine anyone in this country who has not used some type of sports equipment at one time or another (riding a bicycle, playing tennis, taking a hike). Furthermore, in many situations sports equipment is not even used for sports. For example, employees in many professions (nurses, orderlies, waitresses, waiters, fast food workers, carpenters) have adopted tennis shoes as part of their standard uniform because of the comfort they provide, and warm-up suits have become commonplace as everyday wear for many people. "As much as 70 percent of the over four billion dollars spent on sports clothing may be for non-sports use" (Curry & Jiobu, 1984, p. 3). *American Marketplace* (1990, June 21, p. 108) reported that 9% of all women's shoes and 14% of all men's shoes are bought for athletic use.

A recent survey states that "… sports is an element of American life so pervasive that virtually no individual is untouched by it…. (The) United States is a nation of sports fans… (and) sports participants" (Miller Lite Report on American Attitudes Toward Sports, cited in Coakley, 1990, p. 1).

What then is the connection between sports equipment and society? Most sports involve the use of some type of equipment as an essential part of the activity itself. Try to imagine ice skating without skates or playing golf without a club! Even sports that do not require tools to perform the activity (running, walking, swimming), do have uniforms or costumes, footwear, and other supplies.

Many similar sports use equipment that is quite different. Note the difference between: water skiing, alpine skiing, and cross-country skiing; softball and baseball; field hockey and ice hockey. Some of these sports have similar names, yet each is unique, as may be observed based on the equipment.

Sporting equipment is found in every class and society in the world. For years the local, regional, and national sporting goods stores were the primary outlet for sports equipment and supplies. In recent years, however, there has been a proliferation of stores specializing in particular activities or recreational enterprises. Most cities have specialty shops with gear and uniforms for individual activities (run-

FIGURE 1–5 ■ Many fans and the public at large wear sweatshirts associated with their favorite teams.

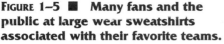

ning, tennis, golf, bicycling, archery, and dance); team sports (soccer, baseball, and football); outdoors, mountain, and wilderness activities (fishing, camping, backpacking, alpine skiing); water sports (canoeing, windsurfing, and rafting); aerobics, fitness, and exercise activities; and so forth.

For many people, the way one dresses to participate in a sport is as important as the utensils needed to play the sport. It is not enough to play well; one must "look the part" also. Sports reporters spend considerable time commenting on how the players are dressed, particularly in announcing womens' sports events (figure skating, tennis, gymnastics). Unfortunately, sometimes the emphasis has been placed in the wrong direction, enforcing the old idea that women had better look good, because they can't play good. This attitude is rapidly changing as women's sports programs continue to expand and society in general becomes more aware of the capabilities of women.

FIGURE 1–6 ■ Sports apparel available for purchase from a discount department store.

Some types of equipment have become associated with particular segments of society. For example, a stereotyped impression exists that blacks and basketballs go hand-in-hand. This is emphasized by Coakley: "It is no accident that blacks in the United States have excelled in sports requiring little expensive equipment and training. For example, basketballs are cheap and the best coaching is widely available in public school programs. Furthermore, outdoor basketball courts are cheap to build and cheap to maintain" (Coakley, 1990, p. 212).

In the same line of thinking, certain sports and sports equipment, originally associated with the wealthy, have become popular with the middle class (tennis, golf, bicycling). In the late 1800s and early 1900s, "bicycling was a particular favorite of many wealthy people" (Spears & Swanson, 1978, p. 147).

Figure skating is another sport that has been affiliated primarily with the higher economic classes. "Figure skating represents an extreme case of how much money a sport can require. Basketball represents the opposite extreme" (Curry & Jiobu, 1984, p. 67). *The Final Report of the President's Commission on Olympic Sports* (cited in Curry & Jiobu, 1984) lists equipment costs for competitive figure skating for one year as $6,000 and the costs of competitive basketball for one year as $30 for sneakers and $0 for equipment the school would provide.

In another example of the sociological emphasis, Coakley (1990, pp. 184–185) states: "… discrimination was also obvious in the realm of facilities and equipment. Women were often given the old gym…. Other hand-me-downs

FIGURE 1–7 ■ Basketballs and other sports balls for sale.

included the old swimming pool, old uniforms from the men's teams, and used equipment. When hand-me-downs were not available the women either had nothing or had to share facilities and equipment with the men."

To correct this widespread bias, Congress passed Title IX of the Educational Amendments in 1972. The purpose of Title IX is to prohibit sex discrimination in education programs that receive federal financial assistance. Title IX specifies eleven areas where males and females must receive equal treatment; one of which is the provision of sports equipment and supplies. A sport program is in compliance (in the area of equipment and supplies) if there exist equivalent amount, quality, suitability, maintenance, replacement, and availability. For further information regarding Title IX, see Appendix B: Compliance with Title IX.

Finally, one of the negative sociological influences connected with sports is the relationship between sports attire and gangs. Unfortunately, due to the popularity of sports apparel and the heroic images portrayed in advertising some drug dealers and gangs have adopted particular sport products as part of their identity.

"'The Intervale gang uses all Adidas stuff, exclusively—hats, jackets, sweatpants, shoes,' says Bill Stewart III, a probation officer at the Dorchester District Court in Boston, one of the busiest criminal courts in the nation. 'They even have an Adidas handshake, copying the three stripes on the product. They extend three fingers when they shake hands'" (cited from Telander, 1990, May 14, p. 43).

These examples show that there is a definite connection and point to ways that society influences sports and equipment and the impact that sports and equipment has on society.

Psychological Influences

Is there any connection between sports equipment and the psychology that is a part of games and activities?

As an illustration consider the following: Teams that appear in attractive uniforms of the latest styles carrying the most innovative implements always draw attention. If it does nothing more than assist athletes with their self-esteem, then that is enough to make a difference to many players and coaches. Furthermore, many coaches use this approach not only to "psych up" their athletes, but also, to "psych out" their opponents.

Merkel (cited in *Team Uniforms*, 1987, January, p. 53) states that "the psychological life that nice-looking uniforms give athletes may provide the winning edge. Winning isn't only based on the coach's strategies, but also how kids feel. If they look good, they feel good and if they feel good, they play good."

Unfortunately, there is a dark side to this element of wanting to look good. A serious problem exists in many cities where young people are attacking their peers over a pair of sneakers or other sports apparel. According to Telander (1990, May 14, p. 38): "In some cities muggings for sportswear are commonplace—

Atlanta police, for instance, estimate they have handled more than 50 such robberies in the last four months." Chicago districts "have had about 50 reported incidents involving jackets and about a dozen involving gym shoes each month."

There have also been killings associated with the muggings. A 15-year-old boy from Anne Arundel County, Maryland, was strangled by his basketball buddy for his two-week-old $115 basketball shoes.

In another incident, a 14-year-old boy was shot to death in the hallway of his junior high school by someone who wanted his silky blue Georgetown jacket. In Houston, a 16-year-old boy was shot to death when he refused to turn over his Air Jordan hightops. One additional situation involved an 18-year-old Baltimore youth who "was robbed of his $40 sweatpants and then shot and killed" (Telander, 1990, May 14, p. 38).

These are merely a handful of the violent incidents occurring over possession of sports apparel. It is a sad commentary that, for some people, what one wears is more valuable than one's self.

Political Influences

What connection exists between politics and sports? In competition at all levels (including the Olympics), "athletes and coaches push rules to the limit and constantly seek new technology and technique" (Curry & Jiobu, 1984, p. 183).

Indeed, equipment is an issue worldwide. The type of equipment allowed for Olympic competition is strictly enforced for most sports. There are some exceptions, however. Presently there are no rules governing the size of tennis rackets being used in international competition. "Not until fairly recently did racket size become an issue. We expect that explicit rules will soon be made to regulate racket size and other technological changes" (Curry & Jiobu, 1984, p. 184).

FIGURE 1–8 ■ Various sizes and types of tennis rackets, which range in the size of the frame from a regular head, mid-size, oversize, and supersize.

FIGURE 1–9 ■ Health and fitness centers compete for members by providing "state of the art" equipment like this weight bench and this computerized exercise bicycle.

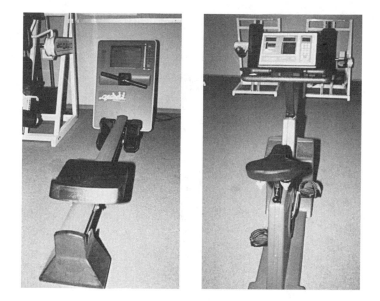

Regulations regarding equipment in many sports are in question at the present time internationally. One example is whether skinsuits should be permitted in swim meets (Curry & Jiobu, 1984).

The types of equipment allowed in competition are major factors among teams of the National Football League (NFL), National Basketball Association (NBA), National Hockey League (NHL), National Collegiate Athletic Association (NCAA), and National Association of Intercollegiate Athletics (NAIA). In competition, everyone wants an edge for winning. All sports leagues

FIGURE 1–10 ■ A computerized treadmill tracks and measures aspects of a member's walking regimen.

FIGURE 1–11 ■ **Computerized components from exercise equipment measure speed, time, power, and other aspects of activity.**

have established strict rules to govern this issue, and continually enforce them to provide fair play.

Equipment is also used for recruiting purposes. Teams entice recruits with the best-looking uniforms, latest gadgets, most efficient machines, quality service, and supplies. Equipment is part of the package when deals are being negotiated.

Fitness and health clubs purchase and advertise the latest, most striking, finest quality exercise machines in order to attract customers. Because it is a highly competitive business, having the most expensive and the best equipment is imperative.

The latest craze is computerized fitness machines: treadmills, rowing machines, bicycles, stairclimbers, weight resistance, and strength training machines. Some machines even provide a printed report at the end of each session showing workout results.

Financial Influences

There was a time when only one type of tennis shoe was available for all types of sports. That is no longer the case—some sport shoe manufacturers make more than 150 different models (Girard, 1988, October).

Sports are big business in today's world. Vanderzwaag (1984, p. 235) notes: "Next to facilities, equipment also has to rank as one of the leading financial concerns in the sport enterprise." Figures from the SGMA Recreation Market Report (Sporting Goods Manufacturers Association, 1989) show the U.S. *wholesale* value of annual manufacturers shipments as: $10,034,000 (sports equipment);

FIGURE 1–12 ■ Comparison of older and newer exercise bicycles. Older bikes were equipped only with a speedometer; newer bikes have ergometers, programmable electronic console, pedal resistance, and readouts.

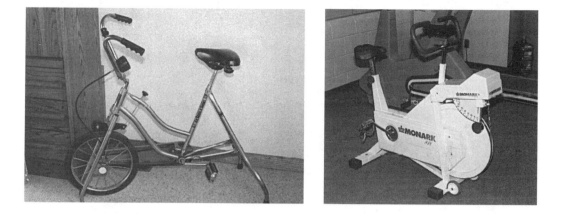

$11,600,000 (sports apparel); $6,970,000 (athletic footwear); and $15,391,000 (recreational transport—bicycles, water scooters, and so forth).

From another standpoint, Legwold (cited in LeUnes & Nation, 1989, p. 414) cites statistics from a New York national information clearinghouse: "1983 expenditures on the part of exercise and fitness enthusiasts of approximately eight billion dollars on activewear, one billion for exercise equipment, yet another one billion on athletic footwear, and $50 million on books concerned with exercise and diet. Additionally, corporate fitness centers and health clubs spent five billion on various programs and paraphernalia to support their operations."

Girard (1988) proclaims that exercise walking is now the nation's third largest participation sport behind swimming and cycling. "According to a survey by NPD/Smart, a market research company, walking is the No. 1 growth category in the $3.7-billion athletic footwear business" (Girard, 1988, December, p. 46).

It is estimated that there are 55 million walkers and 3,000 walking clubs in the United States. There are at least 15 brands of walking shoes and 140 styles to accommodate these participants (LeUnes & Nation, 1989, p. 6). Such an enormous supply has been created to meet the consumers' demands for choices of style, fit, cost, and material, depending on specific use.

Exercise walking has yet to reach its peak. The sport is becoming specialized into fitness walkers, hiking and backpack walkers, race walkers, mall walkers, and so on.

"The newest and fastest-growing group of enthusiasts are the mall walkers. Dozens of malls around the country have organized walking clubs, complete with T-shirts, social hours, and special incentive coupons provided by the mall propri-

EXHIBIT 1–1 ■ **Sample Cost of Intercollegiate Football Apparel***

Item	Estimated Cost of Practice Equipment	Estimated Cost of Game Equipment
Shoes	$39.00	$39.00
T-Shirts	5.00	5.00
Pants	20.00	28.00
Jersey	10.00	70.00 for 2 ($35.00 each)
Socks	2.00	2.00
Supporter	2.00	2.00
Shoulder pads	70.00	**
Helmet	95.00	**
Hip, knee, thigh pads	8.00	**
Sweats	35.00	**
Subtotal	$286.00	$146.00
Total		$432.00

*Costs based on average sporting goods prices.
**Same equipment as used in practice.

etors" (Girard, 1988, December, p. 46). So much interest has developed that at least two major shoe manufacturers are developing a special mall walking shoe (Girard, 1988, December).

A completely different commercial enterprise that spends immense financial resources on equipment, uniforms, and other supplies is intercollegiate sports. This, of course, varies greatly among divisions (NCAA I–III, NAIA, NJCAA), conferences (Big 8, Midwest Collegiate Athletic, Big Sky), and levels of play (college, high school). Exhibit 1–1 gives an example of the costs for intercollegiate football apparel.

Other types of sports associations and enterprises also spend enormous amounts on equipment. When the University of Kentucky developed a 3,500 square-foot fitness center for the faculty and staff, they spent $400,000 of which more than half was spent on new equipment ("Kentucky takes," 1987, October). Another example is the renovation of Joliet (Illinois) Junior College's campus fitness center which cost "$152,000, with the exercise equipment accounting for about $91,000 of that amount" (Yost, cited in "Creatively financing," 1988, April, p. 34).

This book presents four primary areas of financial concern related to sports equipment: budgeting, purchasing equipment, costs involved in the care and

FIGURE 1–13 ■ Examples of fitness and exercise machines: a standing calf machine and stairclimbers.

maintenance of equipment, and using risk management to avoid legal costs pertaining to product liability and to prevent equipment-related sports injuries.

Included in the budgeting process are the concerns and purposes for budgeting, the different types of budgets, effective control methods, and the relationship of sports equipment to the overall program budget.

The purchasing of equipment includes the initial cost of equipment, the replacement of obsolete and irreparable equipment, the replacement of lost or stolen equipment, supplying equipment for expanded programs (adding teams or sports); supplying equipment to comply with rule changes (women's basketball size smaller than men's, width changes for football goalposts), and updating equipment (lighter weight backpacking equipment).

The care and maintenance of equipment includes the repair and reconditioning of damaged and worn equipment, laundry and cleaning, inspection and reconditioning, humidity and temperature control, storage space utilization and storeroom management, inventory and control system, and computerization.

The discussion of legal issues incorporates risk management, rules and regulations, liability factors, NOCSAE standards, safety hazards, and the high cost of a lawsuit.

Administrative Philosophy

The philosophy of the administration determines the basic program offered by any sports organization. That philosophy, which includes policies and procedures, also governs the selection, care, and utilization of equipment within the program.

For example, if the program involves competitive sports and the philosophy is founded on "being #1," then the tools must be adequate to make this possible. Such equipment should be of the highest quality and should accommodate the specific needs of individual athletes. Materials that are inappropriate, obsolete, poorly designed, worn, or damaged will diminish the performance of the individuals or teams. On the other hand, if the program is one with a recreational or leisure emphasis, and the philosophy is based on "equal opportunity for all participants," materials might be selected for durability and versatility rather than using a specific person's needs as the criterion.

Another point to emphasize is that sports and fitness facilities are designed to accommodate and use equipment. From the design stages throughout the planning process, it is essential to incorporate all aspects concerning equipment. For example, when developing a fitness club facility it is important to ask and answer many questions prior to building or renovating:

1. What is the purpose of the facility?
2. What types of equipment are necessary to fulfill that purpose?
3. How much equipment is needed to provide for the number of participants and for different activities and interests?
4. How much space is needed for the necessary equipment?
5. How can the facility be designed to provide adequate supervision for use of the equipment and protection against vandalism and theft?
6. How can the facility be designed to promote risk management and eliminate liability factors?

SUMMARY

This chapter provides insight into the important role that equipment plays in the sports world. We explore the connection between equipment and sociological, psychological, political, and financial influences. Finally, we discuss the impact of administrative philosophy. The following chapters present a thorough description of the process of purchasing, including selection and procurement; budgeting; inventory, control, and accountability; maintenance, storage, and storeroom management; legal liability and safety factors; and trends and innovations.

SELECTED READINGS

American marketplace. (1990, June 21). Vol. 11, p. 108. And in the beginning, our football heroes. (1987, March). *Scholastic Coach*, pp. 68–69.

Bourquardez, V., & Heilman, C. (1950). *Sports equipment—Selection, care and repair,* pp. 1, 28–33, 60, 68, 76, 141. New York: A. S. Barnes.

Brasch, R. (1970). *How did sports begin? A Look at the origins of man at play,* pp. 8, 41–45, 144–163. New York: David McKay.

Cheskin, M. P. (1987). *The complete handbook of athletic footwear.* New York: Fairchild.

Coakley, J. J. (1990). *Sport in society,* pp. 1–18, 184–185, 210–213. St. Louis: C. V. Mosby.

Creatively financing fitness centers. (1988, April). *Athletic Business,* pp. 32, 34, 36, 38.

Curry, T. J., & Jiobu, R. M. (1984). *Sports—A social perspective,* pp. 1–22, 65–84, 183–195. Englewood Cliffs, NJ: Prentice Hall

Equipment and supplies for athletics, physical education, and recreation. (1960). Chicago: The Athletic Institute; Washington D. C.: American Association for Health, Physical Education, and Recreation.

Equipment managers can be certified. (1990, October 22). *The NCAA News,* p. 16.

Ferguson, M. (1990, August). *Athletic Business,* pp. 34, 36–38.

Girard, L. (1988, December 12). Walking with the cardiac set. *Sports inc.,* p. 46.

Girard, L. (1988, October 24). L. A.'s mystique on your feet. *Sports inc.,* pp. 44–45.

Harris, H. A. (cited in Zeigler, E. F.) (1988). *A history of sport and physical education to 1900,* p. 139. Champaign: Stipes.

Kentucky takes care of its own. (1987, October). *Athletic Business,* p. 15.

LeUnes, A. D., & Nation, J. R. (1989). *Sport psychology: An introduction,* pp. 6, 414. Chicago: Nelson-Hall.

Pratt, J. L., & Benagh, J. (1964). *The official encyclopedia of sports,* p. 9. New York: Franklin Watts.

Resick, M. C., Seidel, B. L., & Mason, J. G. (1979). *Modern administrative practices in physical education and athletics,* pp. 254–271. (3rd ed.). Reading: Addison-Wesley.

SGMA recreation market report 1989. (Available from Sporting Goods Manufacturers Association, 200 Castlewood Drive, North Palm Beach, FL 33408).

Spears, B., & Swanson, R. A. (1978). *History of sport and physical activity in the United States,* p. 147. Dubuque: Wm. C. Brown.

Team uniforms: Choosing the perfect fit. (1987, January). *Athletic Business,* pp. 52–53.

Telander, R. (1990, May 14). Senseless. *Sports Illustrated,* pp. 36–38, 43 44, 46, 49.

Vanderzwaag, H. J. (1984). *Sport management in schools and colleges,* pp. 235–236. New York: John Wiley.

Wulf, S., & Kaplan, J. (1990, May 7). Glove story. *Sports Illustrated,* pp. 66–70, 72–76, 78, 80, 82.

Zeigler, E. F. (1988). *History of physical education and sport,* pp. 37–39. Champaign: Stipes.

Chapter Two

THE SELECTION PROCESS

INTRODUCTION

The selection and purchasing of equipment is one of the most important jobs performed by the physical education, recreation, or athletic director (Chapter 1). Practically all of the activities offered in recreational, school, or college settings require the use of equipment. It is the responsibility of the sponsoring organization to provide quality equipment for every aspect of the program. In fact, these programs depend on having an adequate amount of good quality equipment and would not exist without it.

From an educator's point of view, the proper kinds of equipment are essential tools in the learning process. Motor learning takes place primarily through movement. Activities that require specific equipment are usually better learned while using that equipment. For example, basketball can be learned by using a volleyball to practice, but using the proper ball would result in better skill acquisition.

Most equipment, however, is expendable and good planning is required to make sure that proper amounts of the right equipment are available at the appropriate times. Equipment costs are one of the biggest expenses in the operating budget of school activity programs and a great amount of money may be wasted unless equipment is purchased carefully and maintained properly.

THE SELECTION PROCESS

It is essential that every program director know the equipment purchasing process thoroughly and be acquainted with the policies and procedures of that particular organization. The director should also be familiar with as many strategies, ideas, and techniques for purchasing and maintaining equipment as possible. Selection of equipment and supplies should provide an adequate amount of properly designed equipment to allow for maximum learning and participation opportunities. The first step in planning equipment purchases is to determine the needs of the program.

NEEDS ASSESSMENT

A needs assessment is simply a determination of the needs of a program and begins with an overview of the situation. Is the program new or is it already in existence? Is it purely recreational, competitive, or is the primary emphasis on education? The needs for one program may vary greatly from that of other programs. Equipment and supplies required for an elementary school program are different from those needed for high school or college athletics, or for a YMCA/YWCA program. It is necessary to consider the scope, variety, and nature of the overall program. It is very important that the person responsible for purchasing supplies and equipment carefully study his or her own situation and estimate its needs objectively and realistically. These issues are important considerations in any program but especially when organizing a new program.

Available Space and Facilities

The amount and type of indoor and outdoor activity spaces available have a strong influence on the purchase of supplies and equipment. Available activity space and facilities are major considerations when determining what activities to offer in a program. It is not uncommon for equipment to be purchased without taking into account the required safety and circulation space around the equipment. Activity areas become unsafe if the equipment cannot be set up properly due to lack of space.

Also, there is no use deciding to offer swimming classes if there is no pool available! Some equipment is strictly for indoor use and is not appropriate or cost-effective for outdoor use. For example, the use of leather volleyballs and basketballs is preferable in indoor situations; they would soon be ruined on outdoor playing surfaces, which require either rubber or synthetic balls.

Desired Activities

The activities in the program are primary factors in the selection of equipment and supplies. Most activities require unique materials and cannot be conducted adequately without those materials. In fact, there are very few activities that can be conducted without some type of equipment.

Safety and Health of the Participants

Few factors, if any, are more important in the selection, care, and use of equipment and supplies than safety. All equipment and supplies must be selected with this in mind. In any activity involving an element of risk or bodily contact, this is of utmost importance. For example, in selecting football helmets, baseball batting helmets, and gymnastic equipment, the participants' safety must be the top factor in the process. Any attempt to reduce costs by sacrificing safety is completely unjustifiable. It is imperative that protective equipment, meet the accepted standard for safety.

The National Operating Committee on Standards for Athletic Equipment (NOCSAE) is an organization whose primary purpose is to conduct research and establish standards for athletic equipment. They test and certify protective equipment that meets their standards. To date, NOCSAE has been interested primarily in helmet and faceguard safety. These include football and lacrosse helmets, baseball and softball batting helmets, and football and lacrosse faceguards. Also, it is advisable to replace all protective equipment as needed rather than try to get one more season out of an item designed for an individual's safety.

Number of Participants

The number of participants expected to use the equipment greatly influences the total amount of equipment needed. An important consideration is how many people may be using it at one time (peak participation) and how many over an extended period of time.

Cost

Initial cost, length of life, installation cost, availability and quality of service, ease of repair, and ease of reconditioning are all factors that influence the selection process. The most important consideration here is determining what equipment will satisfactorily fulfill the needs of the program while keeping costs to a minimum. Simply buying the equipment that has the lowest initial cost can be, and often is, more expensive in the long run than buying more expensive equipment. There must be careful analysis of all cost factors, including the life cycle cost, prior to purchase.

Staff and Supervision

The amount and types of personnel required and available to assure the safe and successful conduct of an activity must be a factor in the selection process. Some activities can be organized and conducted successfully only under the guidance of qualified supervisors while other activities may require little or no leadership at all. For example, a class in scuba diving requires constant, close supervision, but a recreation center gym that is open for free play generally needs only minimal supervision.

Instructor/Coach Input

It is imperative that the program director or equipment manager consult with those in charge of various activities before making a decision on equipment and supply purchases. These persons should be well informed on the latest innovations and availability of equipment in their areas of activity. There is probably no one in a better position to know the unique problems and needs of each activity. It is often beneficial to discuss the equipment and supply situation with the participants of the activity. Participants of almost any age can make many good suggestions if they are given a chance. It is also good administrative strategy and good for morale to welcome input from all avenues.

Continual Learning

The equipment selection process is an ongoing responsibility. Technology is advancing constantly and new and better products are introduced almost daily. New companies appear and old ones disappear. Products are always changing and it is difficult to keep up with these changes without a concerted effort. A good equipment manager subscribes to trade journals, belongs to professional organizations, and makes and maintains contacts in the sporting goods industry. The equipment manager should constantly examine many kinds and makes of products and even conduct experiments on them. If a product becomes available that is similar to something already in use, a dealer or manufacturer's representative will probably be glad to supply a sample. This sample can then be placed into service alongside of the regular equipment and, through a process of careful record keeping, the two models can be compared as to longevity, durability, performance, repairability, and style. The equipment manager should always be looking for better products and better methods of operation.

Storage

During the purchasing process, the space in which the equipment will be used and stored must always be a consideration. Improper storage of equipment can significantly shorten the life span of certain kinds of equipment. Excessive exposure to weather and sunlight can have a very detrimental affect on many kinds of materials. Equipment made of rubber, leather, wood, and many types of plastics will deteriorate without proper care. These items must be stored indoors with adequate protection from the elements in order to allow for maximum life span. Also, improperly stored equipment may become a hazard or an attractive nuisance and injuries and lawsuits may result. Dangerous equipment, such as trampolines and climbing ropes, should be secured when not in use. It is imperative that all storage areas be secure and accessible only to those with authorization. Even the best equipment is worthless if it disappears.

Ages of Participants

Another factor in the selection process is the age ranges of the participants. The materials made available for the activities must be appropriate and desirable for the age group. Large-sized baseball bats may not be the best selection for use in a middle school physical education class. This is also an important consideration in programs for older adults. For example, when planning to purchase weight equipment for use by an elderly population, it is important to order light weights and in small increments so that participants can begin at a comfortable level and progress as their abilities allow.

Sex of the Participants

Sometimes the sex of the participants influences the selection process. If the program offers both men's and women's basketball, then two sizes of balls must be supplied. In addition to purchasing equipment for activities that have all male or all female participants, consideration must also be given to the many activities in which both sexes participate.

Skill of the Participants

The degree of skill that the members of a group possess may influence the selection of equipment and supplies for a particular activity. In some activities, equipment suitable for a beginning group is not appropriate for those with considerable skill. For example, it may be desirable to start out beginning softball players with larger, softer balls than those used by people who have more experience. It is important, however, to consider the selection of equipment and supplies that promote continuing participation in the activity as individuals acquire skill and competence.

Physical and Mental Abilities

The ability of an individual to participate safely and satisfactorily in any activity is dependent on the individual's physical and mental status. This is an especially important factor when dealing with participants with physical or mental handicaps. The equipment selection process must take into consideration their abilities and disabilities. For further information on purchasing equipment and supplies for the handicapped, consult Appendix A, Sports and Recreation for the Disabled— Opportunities, Equipment, and Resources.

Type of Organization

The organizational setting in which the activity is to take place may have an important influence on the amount and types of equipment purchased. If the sponsoring organization is a school, then it probably belongs to an association, league, or federation that has adopted a set of regulations on the equipment that is used in competition. The director must know these and comply with designated standards. This may not be essential if the activity is purely recreational and informal.

Length of Season

The season or the length of the period the activity will last can have a bearing on the equipment and supplies. For example, if there are only a few days each year that are suitable for snow and ice activities, it may not be justifiable to purchase large amounts of winter sports equipment. On the other hand, if snow and ice are available for extended periods of the year, purchasing this equipment might take priority.

Geographical Location

The location, climate, and local environment are strong factors in the determination of program needs. If the program location is in the mountains where snow is expected throughout the winter, skiing may be a primary focus. On the other hand, if the location is on the coast of Florida, sailing, windsurfing, and other water sports may be more desirable.

Fit

With equipment that comes in different sizes, fit is an important consideration in the selection process. This is especially true with protective equipment. Good quality equipment that does not fit properly not only does not protect but can actually be a hazard. When considering the fit of individual equipment, it is necessary to keep in mind the growth potential of the participants. If participants are in their early to middle teen years, equipment that is measured for each child and then ordered has a good chance of being too small even before it arrives.

Another aspect concerning proper fit is that many programs hand down equipment from one team to the next. An example is a varsity football team that buys new uniforms and protective equipment and gives the old ones to the junior varsity team, and the junior varsity gives their old equipment to the freshman team. The freshman team ends up with equipment originally purchased to fit varsity-sized players. This may be acceptable with certain parts of the uniform but never with any protective equipment. Local sporting goods dealers and manufacturer's representatives can provide assistance on proper sizing.

Inventory

In an existing program, the needs should first be considered and compared with the activities already in place. A determination must then be made as to whether any changes are needed if the program is adequately structured.

The next step in the process is a complete inventory of current supplies and equipment. This inventory should not only count all items but also record the size and condition of each piece. This allows the equipment manager to decide on what equipment is no longer usable, what equipment can be passed on to other teams (i.e., varsity to junior varsity), what equipment needs reconditioning, and what game equipment might become practice equipment.

Careful written or computerized records must be kept of all equipment and supplies. A thorough, periodic inventory prevents overbuying, which wastes not only money but also valuable storage space. When the inventory is complete, the director must compare it with a list of the equipment needed to adequately support the program. This will produce a clear picture, or wish list, of what to purchase.

Prioritizing

Often the budget does not allow for all of the equipment and supplies desired. When this is the case, it is necessary to prioritize the wish list of equipment and supplies. At the top of the list should be equipment and supplies that are concerned with safety. Participant and spectator safety always has priority. The list can be prioritized further from "must have" to items that would be "nice to have." This prioritizing should include consulting the coaches and leaders in all of the activities concerned. The decisions, however, must rest with the athletic director, department chairperson, or program director. For information on budgeting for program setup, short-range purchasing, and long-range purchasing, see Chapter 6— Budgeting Concepts and Principles.

Other Determining Factors

Some aspects of the selection process that are not necessarily associated with the needs assessment include the following considerations and policies.

Quality

Closely related to both the initial cost and the life cycle cost of equipment is the quality of the equipment. In general, poor quality equipment neither lasts as long nor performs as well as materials of good quality. Two old sayings give good advice about considering the quality and cost of equipment: "It only costs a little more to go first class." and "You get what you pay for." Above all, it is foolish to cut corners when purchasing protective and safety equipment.

Choosing A Dealer

It is advisable to purchase brand name equipment only from reputable manufacturers and distributors. Over a period of time, it is likely that the single guarantee of receiving quality products, good service, and fair prices is the integrity of the companies and their representatives. The advice of an experienced trusted dealer can be invaluable. It is wise to check out a new source before plac-ing large orders, either by asking for references or by first placing a couple of small orders to see how this company or dealer works. Local or area companies may provide better service than large or distant sources. A thorough check includes investigating warranties that cover service, repair, and replacement poli-cies.

Service, Repair, Replacement

The selection of equipment and supplies should always take into consideration the availability of repair and replacement services. Will there be repair parts available in the future? Are replacements easy to get and can they be obtained quickly? Will the vendor promptly replace defective equipment? Who is responsible for items damaged in transit? Is there a warranty, and what specifically are the terms? It is always best to ask questions and not to make assumptions.

Standardization

Developing standards for as much equipment as possible is strongly recommend-ed. This means consistently ordering the same color, style, and material of uni-forms. Ordering identical equipment for more than one season makes it easier to replace items and provides more parts with which to make repairs. Standardization also includes purchasing identical equipment that is shared by all sports, such as T-shirts, shorts, sweats, and so on. The desire to standardize should not, however, prevent the constant search for better products and materials to meet the needs and objectives of the program.

Trends and Styles

Styles in uniforms are constantly changing, as are the materials used in their man-ufacture. Reading trade journals, catalogs, and product brochures, attending con-ventions, and talking with local dealers and representatives are ways to keep up to date on the latest in supplies and equipment. Coaches and players are the best ones to consult on this subject. They will be much happier if their advice is at least considered before purchase.

Centralized Purchasing

In the case of school districts, chains of health clubs, or other large organizations, it can be more economical to place one large order for several schools or groups than to place several small orders separately. Often big organizations have a cen-tral purchasing office through which all large purchases must go. Large school districts often standardize much of the equipment needed by all of the schools. Buying sizeable quantities often results in significant discounts from the distributor. Big distributors usually have centralized warehousing facilities that are responsible for receiving, inventory, and repair of all equipment and supplies, in addition to the ordering and distribution.

Ordering Early

Waiting until just before the season to order new equipment can cause problems. There are delays with back-ordered equipment, discontinued items, faulty merchandise that must be sent back, mistakes in shipping, and other unforeseen circumstances. Ordering well in advance of need can avoid many embarrassing, expensive, and even dangerous situations.

Any of the equipment being ordered that is to be custom-made, requires more lead time than standard equipment. Items, such as uniforms, that are customized sometimes take up to twenty weeks for production and delivery. Many organizations make a standard practice of ordering a full five months prior to the date the equipment will be needed.

Equipment should never be ordered on impulse. A careful game plan should be developed and followed and should include, above all, ordering early.

Ethics

A clear-cut code of ethics for the purchaser is essential to serve the best interests of the organization. Manufacturers' representatives, in an attempt to boost their sales, sometimes offer gifts, favors, or special deals to those in charge of purchasing. These offers should not be accepted. All dealings with salespeople and representatives should be kept in the open and all relations should be beyond reproach.

SUMMARY

The job of selecting and purchasing athletic, recreational, and sport equipment and supplies is neither easy nor to be taken lightly. It is critical to the realization of goals and objectives of the program. In small organizations it can take many hours of research, planning, organization, and just plain hard work to do successfully. In large organizations it can be a full-time job for one or even several people. If this task is not taken seriously enough, it can lead to many problems and even lawsuits. The successful equipment manager is well organized and plans for the future.

SELECTED READINGS

Bucher, C. A. (1987). The purchase and care of supplies and equipment. *Management of physical education & athletic programs* (9th ed.). St. Louis: Times Mirror/Mosby.

Cardinal, B. J. (1990). Selecting equipment. *Fitness Management 6* (1). 37–39.

Equipment and supplies for athletics, physical education, and recreation. (1960). Chicago: The Athletic Institute; and Washington D.C.: American Association for Health, Physical Education, and Recreation.

Frost, R. B., Lockhart, B. D., & Marshall, S. J. (1988). Supplies and equipment. *Administration of physical education and athletics* (3rd ed.). Dubuque: Wm. C. Brown.

Getting the most out of your team equipment dollar. (1989). *Athletic Business 13* (8). 35-37.

Hart, K. (1989). Buying new uniforms. *College Athletic Management 2* (2). 8-12.

Horine, L. (1991). Purchasing, maintenance, and security management in sport. *Administration of physical education and sport programs* (2nd ed.). Dubuque: Wm. C. Brown.

Jensen, C. R. (1988). *Administrative management of physical education and athletic programs,* pp. 355–360. Philadelphia: Lea & Febiger.

Jones, B. J., Wells, L. J., Peters, R. E, & Johnson, D. J. (1988). *Effective coaching* (2nd ed.). Boston: Allyn and Bacon.

Railey, J. H. & Railey, P. A. (1988). *Managing physical education, fitness & sports programs* (pp. 203–205). Mountain View, CA: Mayfield.

Roberts, J. (1990). A game plan for purchasing. *College Athletic Management 2* (1). 12–15.

Specifications important in getting what you want. (1981). *Athletic Business 5* (8). 10-16.

Stock up on savings by consolidating equipment purchases. (1986). *Athletic Business 10* (10). 24-28.

Strauf, D. L. (1989). Anatomy of an efficient equipment purchasing system. *Athletic Business 13* (1). 48–54.

Strauf, D. L. (1991). The specifics of specs. *College Athletic Management 3* (1). 8–9.

Team uniforms: Choosing the perfect fit. (1987). *Athletic Business 11* (1). 52–53.

Chapter Three

THE PROCUREMENT PROCESS

INTRODUCTION

The procurement process is that part of a purchasing program that begins with a request for purchase and ends with the payment of the invoice. This process usually begins after the budgeting (Chapter 6) and selection (Chapter 2) are complete. The primary goal of the procurement process is to obtain the desired, high-quality equipment and supplies, on time, and at the lowest possible cost.

It is important to note that there is no single system of purchasing that is best for all situations. Purchasing systems vary from simple to complex and from informal to highly structured. The optimal system for any organization depends on many factors and must be determined by the purchasing agents involved. These factors include the size of the organization and the existing policies, procedures, and bureaucracy of the institution.

Most organizations, especially large ones, have a written reference manual that outlines the policies and procedures for purchasing supplies and equipment. It is vital that those involved in the purchasing process know and understand completely the system in their organization. These policies may be directed by state statutes or local regulations and must be followed. A thorough knowledge of the required procedure is the best way to ensure the quickest, easiest, and most efficient purchase.

In general, there are two common methods for purchasing supplies and equipment, direct purchasing and bid purchasing. Each method has advantages and disadvantages. Most organizations use one or both of these methods depending on the situation.

DIRECT PURCHASING

After the budget is approved, some organizations allow individual coaches to purchase all of the supplies and equipment for their particular sport or activity. The coach is allowed to spend the money as he or she sees fit. It is then the responsibility of the coach to shop around and get the best value. Other organizations may allow individual coaches, program directors, athletic directors, or equipment managers to make small direct purchases only in certain situations. For example, if the purchase is under a specific dollar amount, typically one hundred dollars, equipment may be ordered directly. The advantages of this method are that the coach knows the limits of his or her budget and will usually shop around to find the best buys possible. This also allows the coach to handle quickly, small mid-season replacements or other emergency situations without going through a lot of paper work.

BID PURCHASING

Most large organizations require a competitive bid process to purchase budgeted items. In most of these organizations bidding is a well-defined and highly structured procedure. Basically, this process involves making a list of the items desired for purchase and allowing several wholesalers to submit bids on those items. A contract is awarded to the lowest bidder who is reputable and can meet the terms of the purchase order.

The following steps list the basic bid process typical of a large organization:

1. **Develop a list.** A list of desired equipment and supplies is developed (Chapter 2).
2. **Obtain approval.** The proper administrative personnel must approve or disapprove the request based on need and budget considerations.
3. **Write specifications.** Specifications are prepared stating desired quantity, quality, limitations, and other factors.
4. **Release request for bids.** Eligible vendors are notified and given a time limit to bid on equipment.
5. **Receive bids.** Price quotations from interested vendors or contractors are received.
6. **Evaluate bids.** All quotes are carefully evaluated to ensure that specifications have been met.
7. **Choose vendors.** The supplier(s) with the best combination of price, quality, service, and reliability is (are) chosen to fill the order.
8. **Submit purchase order.** A purchase order is delivered to the vendor(s).
9. **Receive equipment.** The desired equipment is delivered.
10. **Pay invoice.** Once it is verified that all equipment ordered has been received in good condition, payment of purchase invoice is approved and a check is issued to the vendor.

There can be several advantages and disadvantages to the bid system. The primary advantages to competitive bidding for equipment are that it usually results in the lowest cost available to the purchasing organization and that it also produces a set of checks and balances to help ensure that the best interests of the organization are served. Disadvantages include the length of time it takes to get through the bid process and the fact that there are usually more people involved than in direct purchasing, which increases the chances of mistakes.

Writing Specifications

To be successful at the bidding process, the purchaser must be very knowledgeable and aware of the latest products and innovations in the type of equipment under consideration. In the bid system, the equipment purchaser must specify exactly what is to be purchased. Purchase specifications, or *specs,* are written to list, in detail, the quantities, quality, and acceptable standards of the items to purchase. This written description should state the exact number, color, model, capabilities, composition, and delivery instructions.

The specifications must be clear, concise, and well defined in order to place upon the seller the responsibility of providing a product that meets the needs of the user. If there are any loopholes, dealers can substitute items that may or may not meet the standards desired and the buyer may be forced to accept an inferior product.

Clear descriptions of goods that are being ordered list quantity (each, dozen, pound, box/12, and so on), quality, size, color, materials, brand, model number, catalog number, performance characteristics, assembly/installation requirements, and delivery requirements. Acceptable alternatives may be listed to reduce the possibility of purchasing goods that do not meet the needs of the program.

Purchasers often write incomplete specs. If a bid sheet specifies "Brand A basketballs, Model #18—or equivalent," the vendor decides what is equivalent and can substitute an inferior product. In this case the purchaser must determine if the substitute is indeed equivalent to the item specified. If it is not, the purchaser should not hesitate to refuse the item even if the reason must be justified in writing. If there are several acceptable models, they are listed after the first choice. An example is "Brand A basketballs, Model #18 or Brand C basketballs, Model 2BX." In some situations, such as when a league or conference specifies a particular ball, only one model is acceptable. This is written as "Brand A basketballs, Model #18—no substitutions or alternates."

It is often a good idea to list not only the specifications for the desired items but also to list two or three acceptable alternative brand and model numbers for each. This makes it easier for the vendor to shop around and get the best price while still ensuring that the specifications are met.

There is a point at which adding detail to specs can go too far. Too much detail can confuse some vendors and hinder their choices of equipment. Listing two or three acceptable products by brand name and model number can usually avoid confusion.

Writing a clear, well-defined, and complete set of specs is most important in assuring that what is ordered is in fact delivered. Such specifications also allow a fair comparison of bids when the bidder proposes alternatives. Writing specs wisely can help to alleviate other problems as well.

Example 1

Buying equipment in large quantities usually results in a lower price per unit than purchasing in small quantities. To take advantage of these savings, the purchaser must have adequate storage space. Because lack of storage space is a common complaint, many organizations are unable to take advantage of these discounts. One solution is to specify later delivery dates on items that are not needed immediately. If experience shows that only 12 rubber playground balls are needed each semester, 24 balls can be ordered with the purchase order specifying delivery of 12 on August 1st and 12 on December 1st. In effect, this allows the purchaser to utilize the vendor's storage space at no cost.

Example 2

Another advantage to spreading out delivery dates is that the warranty period of the equipment will not begin until the equipment is delivered. If the purchaser takes delivery and stores equipment for long periods of time, the warranties may actually expire before some items are taken from the shelf and put into use.

Example 3

It is very important to get to know potential vendors and find out which are reliable and trustworthy. Some discount suppliers may buy their stock from companies who have had merchandise sitting in some warehouse, possibly for several years. Age has a detrimental effect on almost all equipment but particularly on inflatables, such as basketballs, volleyballs, and footballs. It is generally a good idea to include within the specs that all items on the bid sheet must have been manufactured within the last year.

Writing a good set of specs is especially important if a particular organization uses a generic bidding system. Generic bidding simply means that the only consideration in selecting a vendor is getting the lowest price. In this case the specs must be carefully written to ensure that you get what you really want.

Bid Sheets

After the specifications are written, it is time to submit the bid sheets to eligible vendors. Once again, depending on the formality of the organization's bid process, the bid sheet may vary from a handwritten note to a multipage carbon-copy form. Exhibit 3–1 is a fairly informal bid sheet used by one high school athletic director and sent to at least six vendors. Organizations that require a more formal bid sheet may use one similar to Exhibit 3–2. Often several administrators must approve and sign these forms before they are sent to vendors.

Exhibit 3–1 ■ **Informal Bid Sheet**

1992–1993 Bid Sheet

BASEBALLS   **Price**
   8 Doz.   Diamond D#1   _____
   6 Doz.   Wilson Practice Balls   _____
   1 Doz.   Poly-Indoor Machine Balls _____

BASKETBALLS/LEATHER
   18   Men's Baden BX500   _____
   18   Women's Baden BX475   _____
   12   Wilson Lady Jets   _____

FOOTBALLS/LEATHER
   24   Wilson TDF1202   _____

FOOTBALLS/RUBBER
   6   Full size   _____

SOCCER BALLS/LEATHER
   24   International Brine black /white _____
        or Umbro Ultra #4159   _____
        or Sportcraft #17230   _____
        or Mitre "Nova"   _____

TENNIS BALLS
   75 Doz.   Penn Heavy Duty   _____

VOLLEYBALLS
   24   Tachikara SV-5W   _____

SCOREBOOKS
   6   Basketball/Nat'l. Fed. or equiv. _____
   7   Volleyball/same   _____
   4   Baseball/same   _____
   4   Softball/same   _____
   4   Wrestling/Cliff Keen   _____
   6   Soccer   _____
   6   Tennis/Wirtanen   _____

NETS

1 Volleyball/black nylon/steel cable
Senoh VP 20325

2 pr. Baskctball/Anti-whip

WRESTLING EQUIPMENT

36 Head Gear/Keen M22 "Halo" (white)

24 Mat tape 4" x 84' transparent

36 pr. Knee pads (blue)

FOOTBALL EQUIPMENT

6 pr. Receiver gloves

36 Helmets Pac 3 Riddell

size:	6 3/4	6 7/8	7	7 1/8	7 1/4	7 3/8	7 1/2	7 3/4
amount:	1	3	10	7	11	2	1	1

Helmet Total

150 Mouthpieces— green

100 T-clips

6 Kick-off tees —3 regular/3 soccer style

6 2" Kicking Blocks

100 Laces—36"

12 Scrimmage vests, 100% nylon net, elastic armholes, elastic waist/red only

12 pr. Forearm pads/bluc only

12 pr. Elbow pads/blue only

12 pr. Lineman gloves

12 pr. Hand shields/Rogers #1410101

BASKETBALL EQUIPMENT

1 Toss Back #TB101000

4 Rims (breakaway) Rear Mount

2 Glass Backboards BSN 5028XXX or equiv.

VOLLEYBALL EQUIPMENT

36 pr. Knee pads/Asics Tiger K-05

BASEBALL EQUIPMENT

12 Batting helmets/ABH or equiv./blue
sizes: 6/S   6/M

1 set Bolco bases & pegs

1 Bolco pitching rubber

When the bids come in from vendors, they must be evaluated to determine which will provide the best combination of price, quality, reliability, and service. It is important to realize that asking for bids is not a commitment to purchase. Bid requests are often used to get prices for equipment in order to determine what will fit in the budget. Such recent, accurate information on costs can help generate a realistic list of purchasing priorities.

Purchase Orders

When all of the bids are returned and evaluated, a decision is made on what specific equipment to purchase. The next step is to complete a purchase order and deliver it to the chosen vendor(s). Exhibit 3–3 shows a sample purchase order. The purchase order should include any special instructions, such as delivery date, billing address, installation instructions, and so on.

One strategy that is sometimes used to circumvent an organization's purchasing regulations is called "incremental purchasing." Incremental purchasing is simply the breaking up of one large purchase into two or more smaller purchases in order to bypass the rules that govern single expenditures in excess of a certain amount. Although this may be effective in some situations, it may also be illegal. It is important to know all regulations regarding purchasing for each organization before trying any strategy that may be out of the ordinary.

SPECIAL SITUATIONS

Centralized Purchasing

Often large organizations, such as school systems or state institutions, do all of their buying through a central purchasing office. There are advantages and disadvantages to centralized purchasing. Substantial volume discounts may be available if a school district can coordinate all of their purchases through a central office and have all schools agree on the same kind of equipment. Centralized purchasing can also relieve the program or department administrator of the burden of having to be an expert in the purchasing process, so he or she can concentrate on other duties.

A disadvantage to centralized purchasing is that the person in charge of ordering may neither know nor care about athletic or recreational equipment. It is not uncommon for an organization's purchasing agent to make decisions about purchases without consulting the person who will use the items. This may result in some big surprises from time to time and may cause problems. Usually the purchasing agent's priority is to save money by buying the least expensive equipment available. If the purchasing agent does not have a background in physical education, recreation, or athletics, there is a lack of fundamental knowledge necessary to make informed decisions. Without this professional orientation, a purchasing

Exhibit 3–2 ■ Request for Bids

REQUEST FOR BIDS
Rocky Mountain School District

TO: _____
    Firm's Name

_____
    Firm's Address

_____

_____

RETURN TO ADDRESS BELOW:

Athletic Director

East High School

1721 W. Main Street

East Biafra, AZ 09876

Indicate in the space provided your price quotation for the articles as described. If you offer a substitute, give complete description and pertinent details.

Please return to Athletic Director by _____

Date merchandise needed by _____

Quantity	Description	Unit price	Total
18 each	Baden BX500 Basketballs		
24 each	Tachikara SV-5W Volleyballs		
50 dozen	Penn Heavy Duty Tennis Balls		
8 pair	Pro Swim Fins #552		

Merchandise per above quotation FOB _____

Shipment can be made in _____ days

Terms: _____

_____

Signature _____

Title _____

35

Exhibit 3–3 ■ **Purchase Order**

PURCHASE ORDER
Rocky Mountain School District

PURCHASE	123456
ORDER	
NUMBER	

S
H
I
P

T
O

To:
Attn: Al
Elmers Sporting Goods
4301 Chips Road
Dallas, TX 75240

B
I
L
L

T
O

BUSINESS OFFICE
ROCKY MOUNTAIN SCHOOL DISTRICT
3250 COMMON ROAD
WEST BEEFALO, MT 67111
(444) 681-3256

Date	Account Number	Department	Amount
7/29/92	011-134-020	Physical Ed.	$908.00

QUANTITY	UNIT	DESCRIPTION	PRICE	EXTENSION
12	ea.	Voit XB 202 Basketball	27.00	324.00
4	pr.	Pro Swim Fins #552	14.00	56.00
2	doz.	Wilson TD F1202 Leather Footballs	22.00	528.00
			TOTAL	$908.00

ROCKY MOUNTAIN SCHOOL DISTRICT

RECEIVED BY: _____

DATE: _____

Authorized Signature

agent may make decisions strictly on the basis of economy rather than performance and value. For example, a central purchasing agent receives a purchase request for twenty rubber footballs, and sees in a catalog that one brand sells for $8.95 while another, which looks much the same, sells for $10.95. The least expensive one appears to be the better buy. He or she may not understand that one ball may be slick and another is textured, or that one may not be properly balanced, or that one will better withstand the rigorous treatment it will receive in a particular situation. Of course, a purchasing agent who has complete, approved specifications is unlikely to make such errors.

It is generally advisable to award the purchase order to one vendor who can supply all of the equipment. Sometimes a buyer may split an order to get lower prices on individual items. This may save a little money but that will probably not make up for the headaches it can cause. Not only does the paperwork increase dramatically but problems with the delivery of some equipment are likely. It is much easier to stay in contact with one supplier than to keep track of several. Also, a vendor is more likely to go out of his or her way to give good service to a large account than to a small one.

Continuing Purchases

If a repetitive need for a large quantity of the same item or items exists, it may be possible to obtain a continuing purchase order. Basically, this is an open-ended quantity order that is used to purchase the specified items over a given period of time. This type of purchase order may obtain a more favorable price and reduce the number of transactions.

SUMMARY

The purchasing of equipment and supplies is a vitally important part of any athletic, physical education, or recreation program. The purchasing process may vary from one organization to the next, but the importance of an efficient process does not. There are often different procedures to follow depending on the dollar amount of the purchase. One organization may allow only purchases of less than $100 without bids, while a similar organization may buy all of their equipment by direct purchase.

Making mistakes in the procurement of equipment and supplies can not only be expensive and detrimental to the program, but it can actually be a violation of a state or federal law. Again, it is vital that those involved in the purchasing process know and understand completely the system that exists in their organization.

SELECTED READINGS

Bucher, C. A. (1987). The purchase and care of supplies and equipment. *Management of physical education & athletic programs* (9th ed.). St. Louis: Times Mirror/Mosby.

Dealer or direct? The changing face of athletic purchasing. (1985). *Athletic Business 9* (10). 16–22.

Equipment and supplies for athletics, physical education, and recreation. (1960). Chicago: The Athletic Institute; & Washington D.C.: American Association for Health, Physical Education, and Recreation.

Ferguson, M. (1990). Winning at bidding. *Athletic Business 14* (8). 34–38.

Frost, R. B., Lockhart, B. D., & Marshall, S. J. (1988). Supplies and equipment. *Administration of physical education and athletics* (3rd ed.). Dubuque: Wm. C. Brown.

Getting the most out of your team equipment dollar. (1989). *Athletic Business 13* (8). 35-37.

Hart, K. (1989). Buying new uniforms. *College Athletic Management 2* (2). 8-12.

Horine, L. (1991). Purchasing, maintenance, and security management in sport. *Administration of physical education and sport programs* (2nd ed.). Dubuque: Wm. C. Brown.

Jensen, C. R. (1988). *Administrative management of physical education and athletic programs,* pp. 355–360. Philadelphia: Lea & Febiger.

Jones, B. J., Wells, L. J., Peters, R. E., & Johnson, D. J. (1988). *Effective coaching* (2nd ed.). Boston: Allyn and Bacon.

Railey, J. H., & Railey, P. A. (1988). *Managing physical education, fitness & sports programs,* pp. 203-205. Mountain View, CA: Mayfield.

Roberts, J. (1990). A game plan for purchasing. *College Athletic Management 2* (1). 12–15.

Schlatter, T. (1990). The best in bidding. *College Athletic Management 2* (3). 8–9.

Strauf, D. (1989). Anatomy of an efficient equipment purchasing system. *Athletic Business 13* (1). 48-54.

Team uniforms: Choosing the perfect fit. (1987). *Athletic Business 11* (1). 52–53.

Using competitive bidding to your advantage. (1981). *Athletic Business 5* (9). 27–29.

Chapter Four

INVENTORY, CONTROL, AND ACCOUNTABILITY

INTRODUCTION

The organization's leader, whether department chairperson, athletic director, manager, owner, or other administrative head, is ultimately accountable for all supplies, apparatus, and materials. The administrator must take the lead in establishing policies and appropriate guidelines. Creating an impractical or theoretical system is a waste of time and poor management. A useful inventory system is well organized and easy to operate. All of the staff should thoroughly understand and follow the systematic program. "State of the art" methods should be utilized and constantly revised to incorporate changes in curriculum, budget, purchasing, and so on.

Jensen (1983, p. 352) states that "inventory involves keeping an amount of stock that is adequate to avoid frequent shortages and resultant small orders, yet not so large that it occupies an inordinate amount of storage space." Figure 4–1 is an example of sports equipment in stock.

Equipment accountability is based on properly securing and maintaining accurate records of that stock. An excellent accountability system also saves money for the program by reducing the loss of equipment. Money saved in one area may then be used in another area or may make it possible to acquire additional items to build up the inventory.

Because computers (Figure 4–2) and special computer programs are now a necessity, they should be instituted for dealing with the enormous load of paperwork. They accelerate the process and provide an accurate accounting system. Further information is provided later in this chapter on accountability through computerization.

FIGURE 4–1 ■ Sports equipment in stock.

FIGURE 4–2 ■ Use of a computer simplifies equipment inventory and accountability.

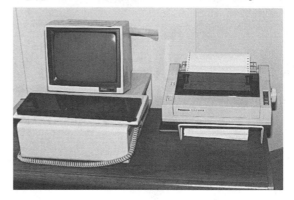

STUDENT MANAGERS

Managing all the equipment for most programs is a very large task, usually too large for the equipment manager alone. When organizations cannot afford to hire full-time assistants, they depend on student managers or part-time personnel. Most collegiate athletic programs rely on students, who may receive assistantships, scholarships, or work-study pay as their reimbursement.

Other programs function with volunteers and interns, which serves as a bonus to the budget. At one university, the equipment manager has one graduate assistant and seven student assistants (on partial scholarship) to help with the equipment. Any volunteers who assist one year are given first chance for scholarships the following year.

It is important to make the job attractive to students, volunteers, and interns, and to acknowledge that they are an important part of the program. The assistants should be self-disciplined, highly responsible, and possess a positive attitude. They must be thoroughly trained in their job responsibilities and should understand their position in light of the entire system (Knickerbocker, 1990, September).

Jeff Boss, as head equipment manager for Louisiana State University, wrote an 87-page handbook for the student football managers. It includes an overview of the student manager's job; rules, policies, and priorities; fitting the equipment; permanent assignments; and work schedules ("Equipment handbook," 1988, October).

Duties of the student managers, interns, and volunteers, may include distribution of athletic equipment; laundry responsibilities; specific team equipment assignments; and repairing, sanitizing, and reconditioning of equipment. Their efforts and input should be recognized and rewarded. They represent the backbone of support for the equipment manager and can save money and provide hours of service for the program.

INVENTORY PROCESS

The system used for storing items can make the inventory process easy. Strauf (1989, January) recommends grouping like items together; hanging all numbered clothing (warm-ups, jerseys, and such); using helmet trees and racks for football gear; and folding, stacking, or boxing other items according to size and style. Figures 4–3 and 4–4 show various sports items placed in storage.

FIGURE 4–3 ■ Two examples of football helmet storage.

FIGURE 4–4 ■ Football shoulder pad trees

POLICIES

To provide a well-managed system of inventory, control, and accountability, the following administrative policies should be considered:

1.   A system of inventory must be thoroughly established and followed.
2.   Everything owned by the organization must be counted in the inventory.
3.   All items that are removed must be officially checked out (whether by staff, students, or clients).
4.   Everyone is held accountable for all equipment and materials issued to them.
5.   All equipment must be coded upon receipt.
6.   Old or damaged items that are being eliminated from stock should be removed only by authorized personnel, and the removal must be noted in the inventory records.
7.   Written procedures must be followed by all persons.
8.   Systematic inventory checks and continual updating must be conducted. The inventory should be kept up-to-date at all times.
9.   A thorough inventory must be made at the conclusion of each season (or other established block of time) in order to know what items are missing or in need of repair and to determine what items must be purchased for the next season.
10. Instruction must be provided on the proper use and care of the equipment.
11. Equipment must be returned in the condition it was in when issued. Upon issue any major defect should be indicated on the record.
12. A system of reimbursement should be established for unreasonably damaged or lost items.
13. Staff members must be aware of the importance of keeping an accurate inventory and of the vital part that they play.
14. A *minimum* number of master keys with access to the equipment room should be issued.
15. Equipment that is seldom or never used should be removed from the inventory. Removal means less inventory to account for and should provide valuable space for other items.
16. Managers should be aware of trends and innovations in the industry.

INSPECTION UPON RECEIVING

Inventory picks up where receiving leaves off. Materials should be inspected upon delivery to ascertain if the amount is correct (compared to the purchase order) or if any damages occurred during shipment or handling (Figure 4–5). The shipment should also be inspected for proper sizes of items and quality of materials. "Boss recommends counting items when they are received and signing only for what is received. If an item being received was demolished during shipment, refuse delivery. And if there is anything missing or damaged, it should be noted on the delivery ticket and the driver should sign attesting to it" (cited in "Getting the most," 1989, August, p. 37).

FIGURE 4–5 ■ **Equipment waiting for inspection and placement into inventory.**

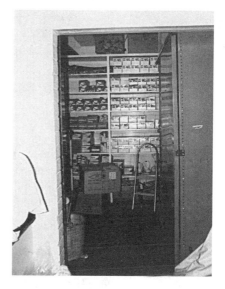

Immediate action should be taken for any problem or error that is discovered. Delay in action can make it difficult to hold the vendor responsible and, as a result, the purchaser may have to absorb the loss or damages. Additionally, most items are ordered with a specific time frame in mind and any interruption will impede the schedule.

All records of the receiving transaction, including date of arrival, should be updated immediately and any discrepancies or problems should be registered on the computer inventory or in the noncomputerized filing system (See Figure 4–6).

FIGURE 4–6 ■ **Example of noncomputerized inventory filing system.**

When this processing is complete, the items should be coded and only then should they be placed in their proper storage areas. There needs to be an area in the equipment room to use specifically for receiving, recording, and coding materials.

IMPLEMENTING AN INVENTORY SYSTEM

In establishing an inventory system:

1. Determine the needs of the organization.
2. Investigate all possible systems that are available.
3. Weigh needs and systems, keeping budgetary constraints in mind.
4. Purchase and emplace system.
5. Train staff on use of system.
6. Create a list of all items in stock and enter into the system.
7. Evaluate amount and quality of items in stock and compare to total amount needed to satisfy program requirements.
8. Order new equipment.
9. Immediately add items received to inventory.
10. Continually update system.

IDENTIFICATION CODING

Establishing an effective method for coding is necessary to preserve the inventory. Whatever type of coding is used, the method should supply all the necessary information and should be used consistently. In addition to the basic identification of the organization, coding can differentiate sports, sizes, purchase dates, and so on. For example, a basketball might be coded in the following way: SPU–MIA–90–1 (Southpaw University—Men's Intercollegiate Athletics—Purchased 1990—Inventory number 1).

Some organizations do not find it necessary to label equipment for different sports or fitness activities because those items are easy to identify. Other sports' programs use a numbering system, based on the participant's assigned number, to mark all articles of clothing, except items that are often interchanged, such as socks, armbands, and towels.

There are many ways of marking or coding materials, however, some are better than others. In determining which method to use, the most important aspect is to provide permanent identification. Also, the date of purchase may be significant for reordering purposes. The standard method is to imprint the name or initials of the organization with indelible ink. The ink should be the type that does not fade or run when materials are washed or are exposed to perspiration or the weather. Office supply stores usually carry a variety of marking pens, most of which are relatively inexpensive (see Figure 4–7).

Other methods of coding include electric marking pens, decals, branding irons, quick-drying enamel, stenciling, and stamping. Another distinction is to use

FIGURE 4–7 ■ Marking net equipment bags for proper identification.

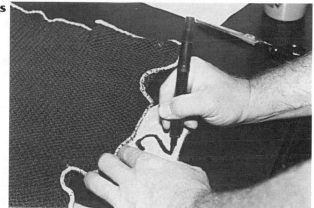

FIGURE 4–7 ■ Marking net equipment bags for proper identification.

different colors of ink. Generally, the simpler the coding method, the better it will work. Two methods of labeling that are usually not successful involve using plain tape or engraving on plastic tape (either of which may peel off) or sewing labels on material (which requires too much time and is difficult to remove).

Helmets may be identified by the manufacturers' codes, which are engraved inside. The helmets also show when they were manufactured, which should be recorded for expiration dates and reconditioning purposes. Short (1989, October) suggests adding extra letters to differentiate between identical codes, which may exist due to different brands. These numbers may also be recorded in the players' computer records to keep track of the equipment assigned to them.

Where items are marked is also important, because visible markings help deter theft. Except in situations where it is inappropriate for the code to be visible, it is wise to place the code in the most convenient position for access by the equipment manager and staff. It is also important to be consistent in marking all similar items.

ISSUING EQUIPMENT

It is important to provide a specific area in the equipment room that is used only for issuing equipment. This helps organize the area and prevent confusion and clutter. Many sports programs provide either dutch doors (Figure 4–8) or garage-type doors (Figure 4–9) from which to issue equipment. (More about storeroom management is discussed in Chapter 5.)

Equipment should be distributed to the users in an organized and standardized manner. Whether there is only one sport or many separate activities, the distribution should be the same. Therefore, it is necessary to design a distribution method appropriate for the particular programs and the types of equipment. The method should be simple, fast, and accurate.

One suggested system is to develop a bar code identification card to give every person using the equipment. In many settings, such as universities and pri-

FIGURE 4–8 ■ Dutch doors used for equipment issue area.

FIGURE 4–9 ■ Garage-type doors used for equipment issue area.

vate clubs, identification cards are required. It would be relatively simple to use the same card for issuing equipment.

Other common systems use identification cards with photos or plastic-laminated cards. Regardless of the system used, the basic information to provide is: individual identification, current membership status (expiration date), and a code number.

Some organizations accept the identification (ID) card in lieu of the equipment that is issued. This is an excellent method when the same equipment is used by many individuals or groups and it is necessary to retrieve those items immediately after a class or training session. When the equipment is returned, so is the identification card.

In situations, such as intercollegiate athletics, where equipment may be issued for an extended period of time (season, year), it is necessary to devise a different system. The ID card can be used to issue items, but it is not kept by the equipment manager. The individual's code number and a list of the dispersed items is recorded. At the end of the season or some other set time, the individual again presents his or her ID and the returned items are cleared from the record. The individual is charged for any items that were not returned, according to the record. The athlete should be charged normal retail prices for the missing items in order to discourage people from becoming collectors. If, instead, the athlete is only charged the wholesale cost, then the institution is placed in competition with the vendor (LaCross, 1989, March).

This method of reimbursement has proven extremely beneficial in retrieving and accounting for equipment, which has been known to "grow legs and walk off" at the end of the season. Other methods used to retrieve materials from students and clients include withholding grades or privileges until the items are returned (see Exhibit 4–1 and 4–2). It is also wise to send notices to individuals a short time prior to the conclusion of the season stating the equipment return dates and listing the equipment they were issued along with the cost for replacement of each item if not returned (LaCross, 1989, March).

Many collegiate athletic programs and clubs use a bag system in which the individual participants are given color-coded (sports are identified by color), nylon mesh bags and large, numbered safety pins. These facilitate the exchange of items that need daily laundering. The participants place their dirty practice clothes in the bag, secure it with the pin, and drop the bag into the "dirty clothes drop" in the equipment room. The clothes are laundered in the bags and then returned to

Exhibit 4–1 ■ **Computer Terminology**

Data base software—software designed to store massive amounts of data, in lieu of a file drawer.

Disk drives—floppy disk drives and hard disk drives store all the information and documents used by the computer. The hard disk drive, usually located in the computer, holds more information, is faster and more convenient than the small floppy disk.

Hardware—the hard elements, such as the computer itself, the keyboard, monitor, printer, and disk drives. Three basic types include the microcomputer (PC—personal computer), the minicomputer (intermediate-size), and the mainframe (large with considerable potential).

Monitor—the screen, similar to a television screen, upon which a document is displayed.

Software—the programming component that runs the system. The program is a list of instructions for the computer (hardware) to perform. Word processing, spreadsheets, and data base represent three types of software.

Spreadsheet—a software program used for working with large amounts of numbers, which are placed in numbered rows and lettered columns called *cells*. Spreadsheets often replace handwritten ledgers and simplify financial accounting.

Word processing —a software program that works with words and can be used to develop forms, statements, or documents. Word processing is a quick and easy alternative to typewriting.

EXHIBIT 4–2 ■ **Sports Equipment Check-out Form**

Team: _____   Team Manager: _____

Date: _____

Uniform #	Check Out	Check In	Comments
15	9/30/93	12/1/93	
17	9/30/93	11/5/93	repair lettering
22	9/30/93		quit team/coach will retrieve uniform
30			
32	9/30/93	12/1/93	

the issue area to be distributed to the user, who is easily identified by colors and pin numbers (Frost & Marshall, 1977). Figure 4–10 shows an example of this system.

Dale Strauf, as equipment manager at Cornell University, adopted a similar system that reportedly saved the university $16,000 the first year it was implemented. "Stauf says that accountability is perhaps the greatest advantage of the pin-bag system. Since the clothes are never removed from the bag, any missing clothes can be traced directly to the athlete" ("In the bag," 1989, May, p. 6). One final note, colored clothing should be laundered separately a couple of times per week to avoid colors running in other items.

It is commonplace in many organizations to require a deposit before issuing equipment. The amount of deposit can be directly related to the cost of the item or items being used. This mandatory payment assures the return of the items or provides the finances necessary to replace those items. For many settings, such as private health or fitness clubs, it may be more amenable to require a one-time deposit, included in the initiation or sign-up fee, rather than submit clients to the inconvenience of deposits on individual items.

FIGURE 4–10 ■ **Mesh bag and pin laundry system.**

When equipment is not returned by a specified time, the individual to whom it was issued should be assessed a late fee. Deadlines and late charges should be posted in obvious places. It is good to be firm, use common sense, and maintain flexibility when dealing with the public in these matters (Beemer, 1989, May).

Another major point is that equipment should not be checked out to individuals who have not been instructed on the proper use of the equipment, including the risks involved in using that equipment. The San Diego Naval Base Fitness Factory has no initiation fees or monthly dues but active-duty members may join "by going through a class on how to use the equipment after being screened for risk factors" ("Fitness finds," 1989, March, pp. 44, 46). An additional area of concern is the fitting of equipment or uniforms, particularly protective gear. This issue is discussed further in Chapter 7.

It is important to establish a simple and secure process for handling cash transactions. All personnel must understand and follow accounting policies for the institution. Employees should not be allowed to accept valuables or other items in place of cash or ID cards (Beemer, 1989, May). Staff members who issue and collect equipment should be highly responsible, trustworthy, and competent. They should thoroughly understand the system and comply with it. A computerized accountability system is ideal for keeping an accurate and well-organized inventory.

ACCOUNTABILITY THROUGH COMPUTERIZATION

Compiling accurate records and systematically updating them is a vital function of the inventory process. It is not uncommon for administrators to spend seventy to eighty percent of their time on such transactions. Fortunately, in recent years, computerization has sharply reduced the amount of time and effort spent on this monumental task. The most obvious benefit is that instead of compiling and maintaining hand-written records and accounts of the stock-on-hand, it is much faster to put all the information on a computer and simply input whatever changes occur.

Computers also provide for the consolidation of information, which keeps records complete. Other assets of computerization in the sports equipment world include: increasing work production, eliminating the redundancy of activities, improving reaction time by collating data quickly, providing a check-and-balance system and audit trail, and helping to cut expenses by using staff more efficiently which may reduce employee costs (Andrus & Lane, 1989, March). Most administrators would agree with Stotlar's statement that "the microcomputer is fast becoming a necessity" (cited in Donnelly, 1987, p. 117).

The terminology surrounding computers can be as overwhelming as computers themselves. The meaning of such terms as *hardware, software,* and *spreadsheets* may frighten some administrators to such a degree that they refuse to use computers in their programs. Refer to Exhibit 4–1 for a basic list of computer terminology.

The computer skills necessary for simple operating purposes by equipment managers can be acquired through a basic introductory computer course. Also, software is available that allows the first-time user to put a program to work in a matter of hours (Tontimonia, 1984, October).

Since it is apparent that computers are necessary and the staff must be computer-literate, the next step is to determine the type of computer and computer programs needed. There are countless name brands of computer products from which to choose and extreme differences in price, quality, and function. Before purchasing any type of computer hardware (computer, printer, or monitor), it is necessary to decide on the software or computer programs that are needed. The software will help determine the type of hardware that will run the chosen computer programs (Roberts, 1990, January).

It is critical at this point to determine how to best use the computer for equipment management. "Rather than simply looking at computerization as a way to expedite specific tasks, which often leads to having several unrelated software packages, unable to access a common data base, managers should think of computerization as an organizationwide information management tool" ("Computers' best," 1989, March, p. 31).

Figure 4–11 ■ Computer data input from the gymnasium.

Would it be possible and beneficial to link the computers between the equipment room and the director's office? Or between the equipment room and coaches' offices? There are ways to provide this service without jeopardizing the inventory records, or accountability measures in the equipment area, or records in any other area. Figure 4–11 shows a computer terminal in the gymnasium that is used to provide or input data and that is, at the same time, linked to the main computer in an office.

An example of computerized use with rosters is that coaches can provide and update rosters at any time during the season (from the convenience of their private offices), the equipment manager has immediate access to this information on the computer in the equipment room, which allows for any necessary changes of equipment for practice or travel purposes.

If there are no computer-literate persons on the staff, it is imperative to consult with specialists in the field to determine the hardware and software appropriate for specific sport programs. If necessary, a consultant may assist with the acquisition process, in which case that person not only should be an expert in computers, but also should have an understanding of sports equipment and the management thereof.

As competition has increased in the computer world, the prices, as with most products, have dropped considerably. Yet, there remains a wide variation of costs depending on the computer's functions. The price, however, should not be the determining factor; rather, the decision must be based on which program will do the job. If the available programs do not match the needs of the organization's operation, it is possible to hire a specialist to design a specific software program. Whatever alternative is selected, it is of utmost importance to review all possibilities and choose the program that will execute as many tasks as possible to perform a variety of services. This makes the purchase cost-effective and, at the same time, assures that the computer and software will be invaluable to the organization.

In addition to the many types of computers (hardware) available, even more numerous are the software programs that have been developed in recent years. There are three commonly known software programs: word processing, data base, and spreadsheets (Roberts, 1990, March).

Currently there are more than twenty companies providing general software packages for the sports industry and at least one company and one university have developed specific equipment room management programs ("Inventory crunch," 1986, November) (see Appendix D). The primary capabilities of a program should include the ability to monitor current inventory status, locate inventory items, control reordering and lead time, produce inventory lists and reports, and provide for forecasting and planning (Falk cited in Donnelly, 1987).

One type of software that is extremely beneficial for an equipment manager is data base software. It stores large amounts of data and provides the advantage that the data can be changed easily. Roberts describes data base software as "a file drawer where many records that have a similar format are stored" (1990, January, p. 52). Sample data might include a roster of fitness club members and their locker assignments. Changes in the personnel or locker assignments could be updated by interchanging names or numbers on the computer spreadsheet.

Kalkstein (1988, July, p. 44) suggests that another use of the stockroom equipment data base "is to maintain an accurate running inventory of the thousands of items of athletic clothing, protective gear and sports equipment maintained in the stockroom."

There are many types of records and transactions that computers simplify for the equipment manager. One example is a spreadsheet for athletic teams to use in preparing and packing equipment for trips. Such a form might include the following information: team involved, list of players' uniforms, audio/video equipment, game implements, dates (check-out and check-in), personnel in charge, equipment or uniforms unavailable for the game (out for repairs), and so forth.

Exhibit 4–2 is an example of a specific check-out spreadsheet (for uniforms only). It is advantageous to use a computer spreadsheet because individual numbers, dates, or comments can be adjusted without changing or altering the entire form. Immediate observation determines the status of any uniform in question. Obviously, this form can be manipulated to include audio and visual equipment or game day supplies or numerous other categories. The larger the operation, the more critical it is to provide a disentangled system. Trying to keep up with numerous sports and multiple arrangements can be devastating for management personnel who are facing the task without a computer and applicable programs.

A computer consultant might also locate and modify software to the management's operational plans. Another alternative is to hire a consultant to custom-design a software package for the sport program. Cheng suggests that this alternative of custom-designing a software package for a specific program also has drawbacks: "It can be expensive and the results will only be as good as the skill of the programmer and the ability of the manager to articulate what he or she wants the system to do" ("Computers' best," 1989, March, pp. 30–31).

Regardless of the computer system selected and installed, it must be user-friendly (easy to use). It should be as nontechnical as possible and should link programs and procedures to menus, which reduces the chance for error. Preprogrammed computer security controls should be included so personnel may perform only specified functions (Daniels, 1988, March). Finally, all personnel using the computer system should receive thorough instruction on its use.

SAMPLE INVENTORY FORMS

Sample forms for the following types of inventory appear at the end of this chapter:

Notification to Withhold Grades (Exhibit 4–3)

Requisition Form (Exhibit 4–4)

Bid Description Sheet (Exhibit 4–5)

Equipment Card (Exhibit 4–6)

Football Sizing Sheet (Exhibit 4–7)

Inventory Card (Exhibit 4–8)

Equipment Order Form (Exhibit 4–9)

Football Staff Equipment Issue Form (Exhibit 4–10)

Equipment Log (Exhibit 4–11)

Composite Sheet (Exhibit 4–12)

Inventory Checklist (Exhibit 4–13)

Sample Order and Receiving Form (Exhibit 4–14)

Individual Roster (Exhibit 4–15)

New Athlete Information Form (Freshman & Walk-ons) (Exhibit 4–16)

Lost Equipment Record (Exhibit 4–17)

EXHIBIT 4–3 ■ Notification to Withhold Grades

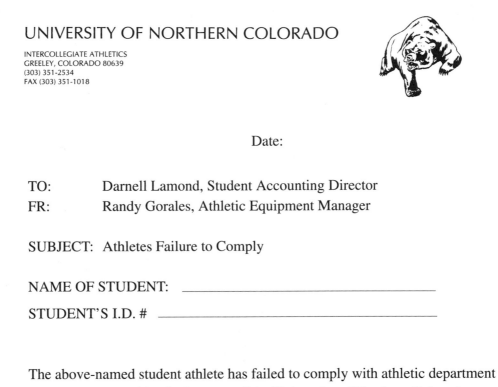

UNIVERSITY OF NORTHERN COLORADO

INTERCOLLEGIATE ATHLETICS
GREELEY, COLORADO 80639
(303) 351-2534
FAX (303) 351-1018

Date:

TO: Darnell Lamond, Student Accounting Director
FR: Randy Gorales, Athletic Equipment Manager

SUBJECT: Athletes Failure to Comply

NAME OF STUDENT: _____

STUDENT'S I.D. # _____

The above-named student athlete has failed to comply with athletic department policy as approved by the Regents of the University of Northern Colorado, which requires student athletes to turn in all University-owned athletic equipment at end of sport season. Please place a hold on his/her grades, transcript, and registration until this matter can be settled. Thank you for your cooperation.

QUALITY • DIVERSITY • PERSONAL TOUCH
COMMITTED TO AFFIRMATIVE ACTION AND EQUAL OPPORTUNITY

Exhibit 4–4 ■ Requisition Form

UNIVERSITY OF SOUTHERN MISSISSIPPI **REQUISITION**
(NOT TO BE USED AS A PURCHASE ORDER) **A**

TO: THE PURCHASE DEPARTMENT DATE _____ PURCHASE ORDER NO. _____

NAME OF ACCOUNT TO BE CHARGED _____ REQUIRED DELIVERY DATE / /

DELIVER TO _____ / _____ TO BE USED FOR _____
BLDG. ROOM

NAME AND ADDRESS OF VENDOR(S) SUGGESTED (IF ANY)

1. _____   3. _____

2. _____   4. _____

DATE PROMISED	SHIP VIA	F.O.B.	TERMS		
QUANTITY	PLEASE GIVE FULL DESCRIPTION AND COMPLETE SPECIFICATIONS ATTACH WRITTEN QUOTATIONS IF SUCH WERE RECEIVED	ESTIMATED UNIT PRICE	ACTUAL UNIT PRICE	TOTAL

UNIVERSITY POLICY: The Purchasing Agent is vested with the sole authority to order materials and contract services. No department may order directly by letter, telephone, or any other manner. The University will honor no obligations except on a previously issued and duly authorized Purchase Order.

CHARGE CODE NO. _____ / _____ / _____ (Account Name and Charge Number Must Coincide)
G.L. Object Dept.

SIGNATURES FOR ALL FUNDS OTHER THAN RESTRICTED	SIGNATURES FOR RESTRICTED FUNDS
REQUESTED BY:	CONTRACT COMPLIANCE:
BUDGETARY AUTHORITY DATE SIGNED	PROJECT DIRECTOR DATE SIGNED
IF PURCHASE OF EQUIPMENT OVER $500.00	
V.P. FOR BUS. & FINANCE DATE SIGNED	CONTRACTS AND GRANTS ACCOUNTANT DATE SIGNED
	PURCHASE REGULATION FOLLOWED:
PRESIDENT DATE SIGNED	
PURCHASE REGULATION FOLLOWED:	PURCHASING DEPARTMENT DATE SIGNED
PURCHASING DEPARTMENT DATE SIGNED	

FOR ADDITIONAL INFORMATION CONTACT: Name _____ Phone _____ Box# _____

WHITE—PURCHASING   CANARY—DEPARTMENT COPY

Exhibit 4–5 ■ Bid Description Sheet

UNIVERSITY OF SOUTHERN MISSISSIPPI

Item	Quantity	Description	Unit Price	Total Net Price
			TOTAL AMOUNT OF QUOTATION	

SEE PAGE ONE FOR INFORMATION AS TO DELIVERY AND TERMS

Exhibit 4–6 ■ Equipment Card

The University of New Mexico	TENNIS	Lock	Locker
Athletic Association			
EQUIPMENT CARD	Date:	SSAN	

Name _____
(Last—Middle—First)

☐ VA.   ☐ FR.

Home Address _____

Weight _____   Height _____

Men's Tennis	Size/Style	In	Out	Charge
Shoes—Practice				
Shoes—Meet				
Warm-up Jacket				
Warm-up Pants				
Shorts				
Shirt				
T-Shirt				
Socks				
Racket				
Bag				

Women's Tennis	Size/Style	In	Out	Charge
Shoes—Practice				
Shoes—Meet				
Warm-up Jacket				
Warm-up Pants				
Shorts				
Skirt				
Shirt				
T-Shirt				
Running Shoes				
Racket				

Check Out

By _____

By _____   Date _____

Check In

☐ O.K.
☐ Short (over)

AGREEMENT: In accepting articles of equipment from U.N.M., I hereby agree to become financially responsible for same and to abide by all rules and regulations concerning use of equipment.

_____
SIGNATURE

Sport _____   Name _____

EXHIBIT 4–7 ■ Football Sizing Sheet

UNIVERSITY OF NEW MEXICO

	Helmet			Shoulder Pad	Shoes	Pant		Jersey
	Size	Front	Back			Waist	Length	

Exhibit 4–8 ■ Inventory Card

UNIVERSITY OF NEW MEXICO

Sport _____

Date _____

Item	Quantity	Unit Cost	On Hand	Disposal

Exhibit 4-9 ■ **Equipment Order Form**

The University of New Mexico   Date _____

FROM:

TO: Athletic Department, Equipment Manager

Item	Quantity	Description, to include Catalog #	Color	Dealer	Est. Cost	PO#	Date	Rcd.	Signature

Equipment once issued to a coach will become the responsibility of the coach, and will be returned to the equipment room at the completion of his/her sport season for service and repair if needed.

Approved by _____   Date _____

Exhibit 4–10 ■ Football Staff Equipment Issue Form

University of Southern Mississippi

Date

Football Staff	Converse Game & Practice Shoes	Game Dress Slacks	Game Dress Shirts	Recruiting Sweater	Recruiting Dress Shirts	Forrester's Rain Jacket & Pants	Suntan Coaching Shorts	Black Coaching Shorts	Black Sweats	White T-Shirts	Oxford T-Shirts	Oxford Staff Shirts	Socks	Hats	Coaches Work Shorts (2 each)	Black Warm-ups	Black Windbreaker
Cary Hall																	
Jeff Bowman																	
Ed Johnson																	
Mike Beller																	
Steve Down																	
Fred Horton																	
Rod Allman																	
Larry Ellis																	
Mark McKnight																	
David Damell																	
Thomas Cole																	
Will Harmell																	
Jerry Gales																	
David Master																	
Doug Randel																	
Steve Best																	

Exhibit 4–11 ■ Equipment Log

Eligibility:

UNIVERSITY OF SOUTHERN MISSISSIPPI

FR   JR   5th
SO   SR

Sport _____   Season _____

Name _____   Number _____

Shoe Size _____ Shirt Size _____ Waist Size _____

Qty.	Item Issued	Date	Mgr.	Qty.	Item Issued	Date	Mgr.

EXHIBIT 4–12 ■ **Composite Sheet**

UNIVERSITY OF SOUTHERN MISSISSIPPI

Name _____ _____ Position ____ # _____

            Last   First

            Waist Size _____ Shoe Size _____

            Locker _____ Serial # _____ Combination ___–___–__

HELMET	Riddell	Shell Size _____	Face Mask _____	
		Frontal Pad _____	Side _____	Top _____
		Back _____	Neck _____	Jaw Pads _____
		Extras _____		
	Bike	Shell Size _____	Face Mask _____	
		Front Sizer _____	Back Sizer _____	
		Jaw Pads _____		

SHOULDER PAD Manufacturer _____ Type _____

                          Size _____ Neck Roll _____ LaPorta _____

                          Extras _____

SHOES	Turf	Type _____	Size _____
		Type _____	Size _____
	Grass	Type _____	Size _____
		Type _____	Size _____

GAME JERSEY Size _____ Notes _____

_____

GAME PANTS Size _____ Notes _____

_____

SWEATS Size _____ Top _____ Bottom _____

GLOVES   Type _____ Size _____

                          Type _____ Size _____

GIRDLE   Type _____

                      Thigh Pads _____ Knee Pads _____ Hip Pads _____

                      Body Guard 34 _____ Rib Protectors _____

SPECIAL PADS a) _____

                      b) _____

                      c) _____

COMMENTS _____

_____

_____

EXHIBIT 4–13 ■ **Inventory Checklist**

UNIVERSITY OF SOUTHERN MISSISSIPPI—FOOTBALL

1.	26.	51.	76.
2.	27.	52.	77.
3.	28.	53.	78.
4.	29.	54.	79.
5.	30.	55.	80.
6.	31.	56.	81.
7.	32.	57.	82.
8.	33.	58.	83.
9.	34.	59.	84.
10.	35.	60.	85.
11.	36.	61.	86.
12.	37.	62.	87.
13.	38.	63.	88.
14.	39.	64.	89.
15.	40.	65.	90.
16.	41.	66.	91.
17.	42.	67.	92.
18.	43.	68.	93.
19.	44.	69.	94.
20.	45.	70.	95.
21.	46.	71.	96.
22.	47.	72.	97.
23.	48.	73.	98.
24.	49.	74.	99.
25.	50.	75.	100.

Exhibit 4–14 ■ **Sample Order and Receiving Form**

UNIVERSITY OF SOUTHERN MISSISSIPPI

Sport _____

Date _____

Item	Quantity	Description	Unit Price	Net Price
1.	15 ea.	Russell #10265 MO practice jerseys color: scarlet with white russ-cote numbers: 12" back & 10" front number/size: 9/XL, 11/XL, 13/XL, 10/XL, 26/XL, 31/XL, 34/XL, 48/XL, 60/XXL, 65/XXL, 74/XXL, 80/XXL, 90/XXL, 91/XXL, 98/XXL		
2.	17 ea.	Russell #10265 MO practice jerseys color: navy with white russ-cote numbers: 12" back & 10" front number/size: 9/XL, 20/XL, 36/XL, 37/XL, 42/XL, 43/XL, 52/XXL, 53/XXL, 54/XXL, 81/XXL, 85/XXL, 88/XXL, 89/XXL, 90/XXL, 91/XXL, 93/XXL, 98/XXL		
3.	8 ea.	Russell #10265 MO practice jerseys color: white with black russ-cote numbers: 12" back & 10" front number/size: 1/XL, 31/XL, 33/XL,62/XXL, 86/XXL, 91/XXL, 92/XXL, 98/XXL		
4.	13 ea.	Russell #10265 MO practice jerseys color: maroon with white russ-cote numbers: 12" back & 10" front number/size: 7/XL, 16/XL, 18/XL, 27/XL, 28/XL, 42/XL, 58/XXL, 63/XXL, 65/XXL, 69/XXL, 75/XXL, 88/XXL, 97/XXL		
5.	7 ea.	Russell #10265 MO practice jerseys color: kelly green with white russ-cote numbers: 12" back & 10" front number/size: 40/XL, 43/XL,51/XXL 86/XXL, 97/XXL, 98/XXL, 99/XXL		
6.	99 ea.	Russell #10265 MO practice jerseys color: gold with black russ-cote numbers: 12" back & 10" front number/size: 1-49 size XL 50-99 size XXL		

TOTAL AMOUNT
OF QUOTATION _____

EXHIBIT 4–15 ■ Individual Roster

UNIVERSITY OF NEW MEXICO

Football 1993   **4/14/93**

1	Livingsten, Mark	33	Nicholl, Dave	68	Deller, Kim
2	Johnson, D. R.	34	Loger, K. L.	66	
3	Thosason, Lane	35	Parkins, Ray	67	
4	Everrenson, Lamen	36	Auvent, Terry	68	Hessen, Mike
5	Enner, Michael	37		69	Desis, Gerry
6		38		70	
7	Braddy, B. R.	39	Dliffin, Brad	71	Levenson, Joe
8		40	Norris, Mal	72	Sillingon, R. T.
9	Bonnet, Rich	41	McCabe, Kerry	73	
10	Penderton, M. R.	42	Baipulu, Stan	74	Chandels, Cary
11	Larant, Jeremone	43	McCarry, Rex	75	Modles, Steve
12		44	Chrisall, Scott	76	
13	Hollingworth, Mike	45	Smith, Daneal	77	Warrington, D.
14	Margin, Bradley	46	Creason, Roy	78	Pettin, Stu
15		47	Turnnet, Rusty	79	Mossin, Eric
16	Goodson, Nate	48	Gorinton, Don	80	Schultin, Evert
17		49	Hantly, Justin	81	Wilson, M. L.
18		50		82	
19		51		83	Brotton, Larry
20		52	Jestinn, Bill	84	Dalen, Levi
21	Winslow, Carl	53	Zinnel, Doug	85	Gromine, Brian
22		54		86	Brown, Chad
23	Gerrett, Aaron	55		87	
24	Woodens, Bill	56	Falk, Chris	88	Sunner, Harry
25	Hennesy, Drew	57	Danils, Ray	89	Planter, Joe
26	Creston, Andre	58	Barry, T. S.	90	Edgley, Monte
27	Terrance, Stan	59	Slanten, Jeremy	91	Chavesen, Ben
28	Davison, Lamont	60	Henderton, M.	92	Carver, Luke
29	Phinston, Juan	61		93	Jeffen, Jay
30	Youngly, Fred	62	Ojeha, Clark	94	Velardin, Kim
31		63	Luanket, Tanner	95	Emerson, Winston
32	Phillings, Richard	64	Clarin, Eugene	96	Vaughing, Kale

EXHIBIT 4–16 ■ **New Athlete Information Form**

UNIVERSITY OF SOUTHERN MISSISSIPPI—FOOTBALL

Social Security Number _____

Name _____

Home Address _____
                        Street   City   State/Zip Code

Home Phone Number (_____)_____

Parent's Name _____

Parent's Address _____

Height _____ Weight _____ Shoe Size _____ High or Low _____

On these items, please try to use a number to indicate your size:

Waist Size_____ Football Pants _____ — Regular or Long _____

T-Shirt _____ Football Jersey _____ Coat Size _____

Helmet Size _____ Hat Size _____

Supporter (Circle One)   Small _____ Medium _____ Large _____ X-Large _____

Practice Shorts (Circle One)   Small _____ Medium _____ Large _____ X-Large _____

Sweatpants (Circle One)   Small _____ Medium _____ Large _____ X-Large _____

Sweat top (Circle One)   Small _____ Medium _____ Large _____ X-Large _____

List any braces needed _____

List any other special equipment you may need _____

_____   _____
Signature   Date

Exhibit 4–17 ■ **Lost Equipment Log**

UNIVERSITY OF NEW MEXICO

Sport _____

Name	Equipment Lost	Date Lost	Amount Owed	Amount Paid	Date Paid	Verification

SUMMARY

This chapter emphasizes the importance of creating a practical and accurate inventory system. Principles and policies for the management of such a program are suggested. Various aspects of the inventory process are stressed, including starting an inventory system; receiving, issuing, and coding equipment; and accountability through computerization. Emphasis is placed on the necessity of up-to-date records, well-trained staff, and high security and controls. A variety of inventory forms are included as samples.

SELECTED READINGS

Andrus, S., & Lane, S. A. (1989, May). Athletic Software Programs. *College Athletic Management,* pp. 34–36.

Andrus, S., & Lane, S. A. (1989, March). Computerizing the athletic department. *College Athletic Management,* pp. 30–34.

Beemer, R. (1989, May). Checking it out. *College Athletic Management,* pp. 62–63.

Computers' best use is in information management. (1989, March). *Athletic Business,* pp. 28, 30–31.

Daniels, M. A. (1988, March). Taking the step into computerization. *Athletic Business,* pp. 44–46, 48.

Donnelly, J. E. (Ed.) (1987). Using microcomputers in physical education and the sport sciences, pp. 124–127. Champaign: Human Kinetics Publishers.

Equipment handbook is student manager bible. (1988, October). *Athletic Business,* pp. 30–38.

Fitness finds niche at San Diego Naval Base. (1989, March). *Athletic Business,* pp. 42–44, 46.

Falk, H. (1983). *Handbook of computer applications for the small or medium-sized business.* Radnor, PA: Chilton Book.

Frost, R. B., & Marshall, S. T (1977). *Administration of physical education and athletics,* p. 335. (2nd ed.). Dubuque, Iowa: Wm. C. Brown.

Getting the most out of your team equipment dollar. (1989, August). *Athletic Business,* pp. 35–37.

In the bag. (1989, May). *College Athletic Management,* p. 6.

The inventory crunch—and how to deal with it. (1986, November). *Athletic Business,* pp. 44–47.

Jensen, C. R. (1988). *Administrative management of physical education and athletic programs,* pp. 352–356. Philadelphia: Lea & Febiger.

Kalkstein, P. (1988, July). The computer can be a powerful (and friendly) tool. *Athletic Business,* pp. 42–45.

Knickerbocker, B. (1990, September). *College Athletic Management,* pp. 20–21.

LaCross, D. (1989, March). A place for everything. *College Athletic Management,* pp. 13–15.

Roberts, J. (1990, January). Spreadsheet inventory. *Athletic Business,* pp. 52–56.

Roberts, J. (1990, March). Equipping the computer. *College Athletic Management,* pp. 9–10, 12.

Short, M. (1989, October). Label laws. *College Athletic Management,* pp. 6–7.

Strauf, D. L. (1989, January). Anatomy of an efficient equipment purchasing system. *Athletic Business,* pp. 48, 50–54.

Tontimonia, T. L. (1984, October). Choosing a computer that fits your needs. *Athletic Business,* pp. 32, 34–37.

Turner, E. T., Tugman, B., & Townsend, T. (1974, October). Physical education equipment personnel—Attitudes, opinions, and responsibilities. *The North Carolina Journal,* pp. 19–20.

Chapter Five

MAINTENANCE, STORAGE, AND STOREROOM MANAGEMENT

INTRODUCTION

It is obvious that equipment accounts for a large portion of the budget. It is imperative to maintain such an investment in the best possible manner. Proper maintenance and storage is also important to make sure the equipment is safe and reliable (see Figure 5–1). Day-to-day maintenance prolongs the life of materials and ensures the utmost return for the dollars invested. Repairing and cleaning items immediately upon return guarantees that they are always ready for use. It should be common practice to inspect equipment at the time of issue and return. All types of equipment, whether large or small, issued or not, should always be in top working condition.

A major function is to provide enough storage space to stock and maintain the equipment (Figure 5–2). It is not uncommon to find little or no storage space, even when facilities are built. This seems to be an area that is frequently eliminated or severely cut when funds run short during the building process. And, yet, this is an essential area; storage has a big impact on athletic programs.

As any equipment manager will acclaim, inadequate storage space has a tremendous effect on storeroom management and, ultimately, on the entire organization. Too many items placed in too small a space creates havoc. Not only is it virtually impossible to maintain an inventory, but it is also like trying to find "a needle in a haystack."

FIGURE 5–1 ■ Equipment maintenance area.

FIGURE 5–2 ■ Storage area providing adequate space.

GENERAL POLICIES

The following policies help provide a storeroom that is well managed and in which equipment and materials are properly maintained:

1. Adequate storage space must be provided.
2. Continual and periodic checks should be conducted to discover items in need of repair and/or cleaning.
3. Written policies and procedures should be followed by all personnel.
4. Only authorized personnel should be given keys and allowed access to the storage or repair area.
5. Continual evaluation and routine maintenance must be done on all equipment that exposes users to risks; the more dangerous the equipment, the more often and carefully it should be checked.
6. Wet uniforms or other items should be dried immediately after usage. Wet equipment used in contests involving travel should be packed separately and dried without delay upon return.
7. Travel equipment should be packed in trunks or specially designed cartons, which assures that the equipment will arrive in good condition. See Figures 5–3 and 5–4 for examples of trunks prepared for travel. Each container should be marked with the contents and an inventory of the items should be made and verified prior to leaving and upon return from trips.
8. Equipment should always be put away clean, dry, and in top condition.
9. Off-season equipment should be stored in a separate locked area that is cool, dry, and well-ventilated.

FIGURE 5–3 ■ Equipment trunks prepared for travel.

FIGURE 5–4 ■ Maintenance kit prepared for travel.

FIGURE 5–5 ■ **Well-organized storage area.**

FIGURE 5–6 ■ **Numerous ice skates stored in an orderly manner.**

10. The entire storage and repair area must be kept clean and orderly with all items stored in their designated places (Figures 5–5 and 5–6).
11. The manufacturer's recommendations for washing or dry cleaning must be followed. Stains should be treated prior to laundering and colors should not be mixed. Using hot water will set stains and create shrinkage.
12. Garments should be completely dry before folding, packing, or storing. Also, wet items should never be hung on iron hangers or nails.
13. A high-level security system, such as an electronically controlled setup, should be installed. This should be incorporated into the original design of the facility, if possible (Figure 5–7).
14. The organization's administrator should appoint one individual to serve as equipment manager, the primary agent for all equipment matters.

FIGURE 5–7 ■ **Surveillance camera as part of a security system.**

■

EXHIBIT 5–1   ■ **Recommendations for Sports Equipment Storage Space**

1938—Apparatus storage room—400 square feet (Evenden, Strayer, & Englehardt)

1961—Space for lockers, showers, toweling rooms, equipment storage, supply rooms, and offices—approximately 40 percent of the play or activity area in a gymnasium facility (Sapora & Kenney)

1967—A reasonable standard for determining the space needed for lockers, showers, toweling rooms, equipment storage, supply rooms, and offices—approximately 35 percent of the activity area in a gymnasium facility (National Facilities Conference Space Standards)

1968—250–300 square feet for each exercise area in the facility (Recommended Ancillary Space from the College and University Facilities Guide)

1988—Recommended Ancillary Space—20-22 percent of the activity space (Walker)

SPACE REQUIREMENTS

How much space should be provided for equipment storage? Obviously, this is a difficult question to answer due to the innumerable differences in types, sizes, and amounts of equipment to store. A recent research study (Walker, 1989) on physical education and athletic space revealed the average amount of storage space at eighteen colleges and universities within two intercollegiate athletic conferences to be 2,857 square feet (Rocky Mountain Collegiate Athletic Conference) and 3,120 square feet (Midwest Collegiate Athletic Conference). Based on these calculations, which were adequate for the storage needs of these schools, the recommendation for sports equipment storage space is 20-22 percent of the sports activity space in the facility. Exhibit 5–1 is a list of past recommendations for sports equipment storage space.

The American Entrepreneurs Association's investigation on physical fitness centers reported that the square footage of a facility should be based on the size of the nearby population and recommended: 1,000–3,000 square feet for 10,000 to 100,000 people; 1,500–4,000 square feet for a population range of 100,000 to 200,000; and 2,000–10,000 square feet for populations over 200,000 (and depending on the type of equipment). Further, the workout equipment space should represent from 50 to 60 percent of this floor space (American Entrepreneurs, 1980). No figures were presented for equipment storage, however.

EQUIPMENT ROOM DESIGN

The equipment room should be located adjacent to a corridor and near locker rooms and activity areas. There should be direct access to a service entrance for transporting equipment to and from the main site. The service entrance needs to have double–wide doors with high clearance (Figure 5–8) for transporting large

FIGURE 5–8 ■ Double-wide doors with high clearance for transporting large pieces of equipment in and out of the building.

FIGURE 5–9 ■ Example of an equipment dolly used for transporting large pieces of equipment.

pieces of equipment, such as volleyball standards and gymnastics apparatus, as well as for replacement of large capacity washers and dryers in the laundry area. Ramps facilitate movement of carts, dollies (Figure 5–9), and large equipment, and expedite the loading and unloading of supplies and travel provisions.

The equipment room should be spacious without wasting space. It must be large enough to hold all the equipment needed to accommodate the sports and recreational activities for an organization, with the only exceptions being large gymnasium apparatus (Figure 5–10) or outdoors sports equipment. The room should include the following: distribution counter with computer space, laundry

FIGURE 5–10 ■ Gymnastics equipment requires a large storage space.

FIGURE 5–11 ■ Different sizes of storage units.

area, equipment storage shelving units or areas (Figures 5–11), repair and maintenance area with service sink, manager's office, and, if possible, a staff lounge
area.

Security is always an important element to consider. There should be no exte-
rior windows in the equipment room. Doors should be solid with heavy locks.
Walls must rise to the floor above or the roof without artificial ceilings, which can
be easily removed. It is advisable to install a security alarm system.

Additionally, the number of keys distributed to staff for access to the equipment room should be limited to the smallest number possible. Proper staff
scheduling will assure that trained personnel are always available to assist and the
equipment area is accessible at all times.

There is no established sports equipment room design that would be appropriate for all institutions and/or organizations. Any particular group must create a
plan to best serve their program. It is important to involve equipment personnel in
the development of the equipment room design. They have specific needs and are
able to provide valuable information critical to the design. In some cases, it may
be best to hire a professional consultant to design the basic layout. Exhibit 5–2 is
an example of an equipment room design.

EQUIPMENT MANAGER'S OFFICE

The equipment supervisor should have a separate office adjacent to the general
equipment area with three doorways. One doorway should provide access to the

EXHIBIT 5–2 ■ Sample Design of an Equipment Room

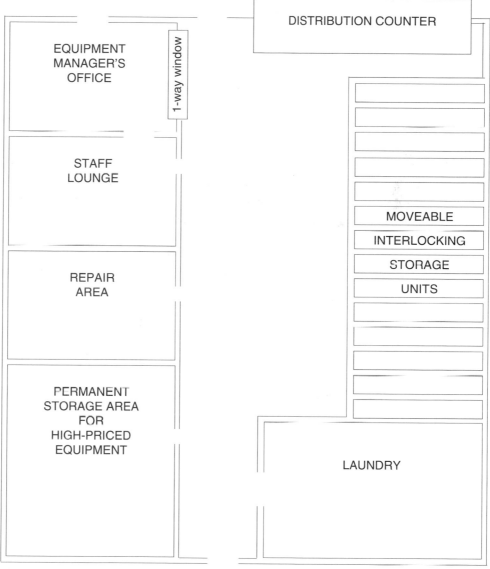

DOUBLE-WIDE ENTRANCE

equipment room and another should lead to an outside entrance to the building, if possible. This allows direct passage for sales representatives and suppliers to meet with the equipment manager without entering the general equipment area.

The third doorway should lead to an adjoining lounge and reception area. This room would provide a place to discuss business in a relaxed atmosphere or to have lunch or take work breaks. Providing such a place has a positive impact on the performance of the staff and their quality of work. The room should have a sink, microwave, small refrigerator, storage cabinets, sofa, and a table and chairs.

The manager's office should be large enough to provide space for a desk, two chairs, filing cabinets, bookshelves, and a computer and printer stand. It should be equipped with telephone and computer lines and an intercommunication system.

The wall adjoining the manager's office and the general equipment area should contain a large window to allow general supervision of the operation. Privacy could be assured by adding one–way see–through glass or blinds.

STORAGE UNITS

Maximum space efficiency may be provided by building functional shelving. Although there are many designs of basic shelving units, it is critical that the unit be appropriate for the specific needs of the program, and that the shelving be adjustable to accommodate varying sizes and shapes.

Exhibit 5–3 is an example of a well-designed interlocking off-season storage system that is organized, easy to use, and secure. The entire storage system may be built for a reasonable amount. Any number of units within the system may be built depending on the needs of the organization's programs and space.

Each unit is classified by two removable cards (which can be replaced if the curriculum changes) placed on the side of the unit that faces outward (see Exhibit 5–4). One card, written in large letters, identifies the sport for which equipment is being stored. One or more units may be assigned per sport depending on the space available and the number of programs. The second card is a computer printout of

Exhibit 5–3 ■ Interlocking Storage System

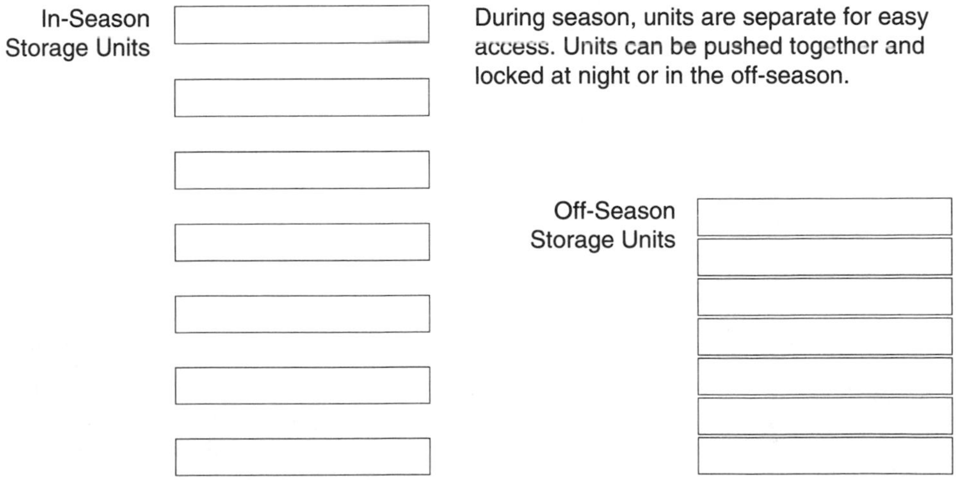

In-Season Storage Units

During season, units are separate for easy access. Units can be pushed together and locked at night or in the off-season.

Off-Season Storage Units

EXHIBIT 5–4 ■ Interlocking Storage System—End View

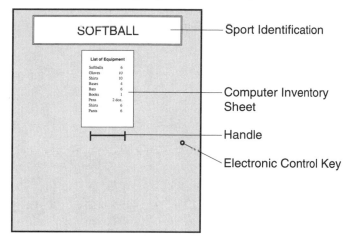

the inventory that is stored in that unit. This card must match the computerized inventory at all times and must be kept up to date.

If even one item is removed or added to the unit, the information is immediately updated on the computer and a copy of the new inventory (for that unit only) is printed. This copy replaces the old inventory sheet which is posted on the side of the unit. The system is similar to that of a library card catalogue. Whether items are removed for repair, issue, or replacement, there is always an accurate count of the stock. Being able to locate articles quickly and easily is a big aid to the equipment manager and staff. It is also an advantage to know the exact count for any item at any time.

The entire set of units may be controlled electronically (or otherwise) from one area and should be kept locked at all times, except for inventory adjustments or seasonal changes. A limited number of personnel should have access to the electronic controls, usually only the equipment manager and the administrative head. Obviously, this system, with very few adjustments, could also be used for in-season equipment. For security reasons, it is best to keep in-season and off-season units separate, with the off-season constantly locked and the in-season locked at night and on the weekends.

Figure 5–12 shows the off-season equipment storage in a separate, electronically controlled area. The individual sliding shelf units are equipped with rollers and/or a rail-and-track system so the entire unit is easily moved from off-season to in-season areas, or vice versa. Lateral movement occurs between the two control areas. After moving a unit from one area to the other, it is merely locked into the corresponding rail system and is restricted to forward or backward movement along the rail.

FIGURE 5–12 ■ A well-designed storage
unit with moveable sections.

EXHIBIT 5–5 ■ Interlocking Storage
System—Top and Side Views Before and
After Units Are Removed

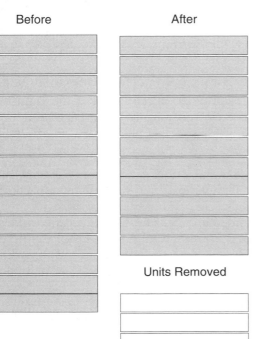

TOP VIEW

Before   After

Units Removed

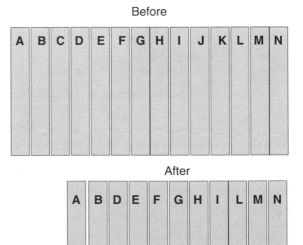

SIDE VIEW

Before

| A | B | C | D | E | F | G | H | I | J | K | L | M | N |

After

| A | B | D | E | F | G | H | I | L | M | N |

Shaded areas represent units locked in place.

For example, with a rail-and-track storage system, as softball season approaches, it is easy to transfer the storage unit from the off–season equipment area to the current–season equipment area. The off–season storage area would be unlocked, unit "C" (which contains women's softball equipment) would be pulled on the rail into the current–season storage area, where it would be locked into place. The off–season equipment area would then be pushed together to eliminate the area vacated by unit "C" and would once again be locked into place (see Exhibit 5–5).

The rail-and-track system, which works similar to a roller coaster or electronic train system, must be laid beneath the floor level with the top of the rail flush with the floor. It should be an enclosed rail system to protect it, keep it clean, and prevent people from tripping on it. Obviously, it would be easiest to build this system when the facility is under construction; however, it is certainly feasible to install it later. It is possible to design and build either a manually controlled system or, if more money is available, an electronically controlled system. Either system is very functional and provides an excellent method for storing and moving large quantities of equipment.

OTHER TYPES OF STORAGE

Nonstackable Storage

Equipment that does not stack well, such as balls, bats, hockey sticks, skis and poles, can be easily stored in bins, canisters, or other receptacles (Figures 5–13). Hanging storage should be provided for uniforms and materials that wrinkle if folded (Figure 5–14). The units in Exhibits 5–3, 5–4, and 5–5 are designed with hanging storage areas and shelves for stacking. Helmets may be stored on hooks attached to the wall or ceiling (Figure 5–15).

Large, Near–site Storage

If appropriate and adequate space is available, it is better to provide storage for large equipment near the site at which it will be used. Near-site storage should be provided for gymnastics apparatus (Figure 5–16); aquatics supplies and accessories (Figure 5–17); portable scoreboards and timing devices (Figure 5–18); standards for volleyball, badminton, and tennis (Figure 5–19); and other materials that require a lot of space (Figure 5–20).

Whenever possible, it is best to provide separate storage areas (with large doors for easy access) near the football field, tennis courts, track area, baseball and softball fields to store the large equipment used in these sports (blocking sleds, dummies, ball–throwing machines, hurdles, portable jumping pits, and so on) (Figure 5–21).

FIGURE 5–13 ■ Storage of differently shaped equipment in bags, bins, carts, and on poles.

FIGURE 5–14 ■ Storage of fencing jackets and masks.

FIGURE 5–15 ■ Storage of football
helmets and shoulder pads on hooks in
walls and ceilings.

FIGURE 5–16 ■ Storage space is needed
for gymnastics apparatus.

FIGURE 5–17 ■ Special devices may be developed to store aquatics materials, such as lane
ropes (left) and pool covers (right).

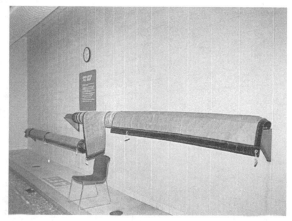

FIGURE 5–18 ■ A portable timing device used for swimming.

FIGURE 5–19 ■ Standards require a considerable amount of space.

FIGURE 5–20 ■ Large equipment items require substantial space to store.

FIGURE 5–21 ■ Portable jumping pits used for track require an enormous amount of storage space.

Small, Near–site Storage

It is advisable to provide a place near activity areas for small equipment that might otherwise have to be carried for long distances (racquets, balls, gloves). For example, Figures 5–22 and 5–23, show two ways to store aquatics materials.

One storage accommodation that is sometimes provided to athletes or clients is installation near activity areas of lockers that hold small items such as keys, glasses, and billfolds (Figure 5–24).

FIGURE 5–22 ■ Storage benches in the pool area serve a dual purpose: storage and seating.

FIGURE 5–23 ■ Kick-boards for swimming are easily stored on shelves.

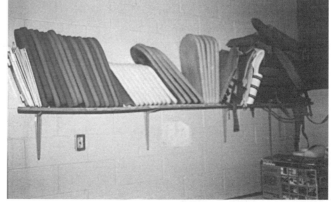

FIGURE 5–24 ■ Small locker space near activity areas.

Outdoors Sports Storage

All types of equipment for outdoor sports should be placed inside for protection in the off–season, when they are not in use. This greatly extends the durability and assures the maximum life of the items. Well–secured areas are necessary for off–season storage. Figures 5–25 and 5–26 are examples of secure equipment areas.

Athletic Team Storage

A totally different system of storage may be necessary to provide athletic gear for a team. For example, shoes, socks, and supporters may be provided to an athletic team but would not be supplied to the general physical education or recreational clientele. Equipment storage areas for many athletic programs provide separate, numbered cubicles for each person's clothing and shoes. These cubicles can be opened from the front by keys or locks that are given to the athletes (Figure 5–27). The backside of the cubicles open into the equipment room, allowing access for stocking the athletes' uniforms (Figure 5–27). Each cubicle is marked with a number that corresponds to the athletes' jersey numbers. All items issued to athletes also carry their jersey numbers. This is a simple, fast, and efficient method of stocking.

FIGURE 5–25 ■ **Well-secured storage area designed for track equipment.**

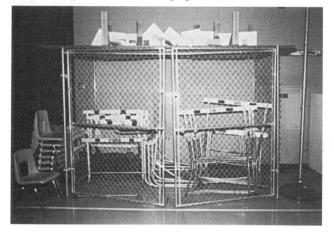

FIGURE 5–26 ■ **Highly secured equipment area.**

FIGURE 5–27 ■ **Athletic team cubicles for each athlete's clothing and shoes.**

Front view

Back view

Corporate Fitness Centers Storage

Most corporate fitness centers are relatively small because they are usually located in or near office buildings (for convenience to clients during lunch-hour, to allow for a maximum workout in a minimum of time). Usual facilities include an indoor running track, aerobic conditioning equipment, and weight machines. Although not as common, some corporate fitness centers include swimming pools, gymnasiums, and/or racquetball courts.

Due to the variety of activities available, equipment storage requirements might include areas for: equipment issue, towel and laundry service, and maintenance and repair. Some fitness centers provide members with gym clothes, locks, or other miscellaneous gear and, therefore, have to furnish suitable storage. Obviously, individual lockers must be provided (Figure 5–28).

Private Club and Spa Storage

As mentioned, the same types of storage areas would be required in private clubs for playing racquetball, tennis, or for general fitness: equipment issue, towel and laundry service, individual lockers for clients, and maintenance and repair. Specifically, the equipment issue storage area would have to be large enough to store mats, jump ropes, weight belts, lightweight dumbbells, rebounders, and other aerobic conditioning equipment.

An additional storage area that many private fitness clubs and spas need is a location for a sales display or "pro" shop. This site should provide a place for stocking and selling club merchandise (imprinted sports apparel, gym bags, exercise apparel, and other such paraphernalia).

FIGURE 5–28 ■ Private individual lockers for members and personnel.

Audio–visual Storage

A separate area should be designated specifically for audio–visual items. It should be accessible, well–protected, and secure. There should be storage room for a moveable cart to transport the equipment easily and to reduce damage due to mis-handling (Flynn, 1985).

Audio–visual materials may also be stored in built–in areas at instructional sites. Turner and McDaniel (1990, September, p. 20) describe a multimedia center at Appalachian State University, North Carolina, called STILC (Skill and Technique Instructional Learning Center), which provides easy access and immediate use by faculty and students for classroom, laboratory, or study sessions. The teaching/learning center is equipped with projectors, screens, videotapes and decks, viewing areas, books, cameras, and related equipment. There is also an area to store unusual sports equipment items used for teaching purposes, such as basketballs with layers exposed, and other specialized teaching equipment. Brochures and catalogs from equipment manufacturers are also available through this center.

LAUNDRY AREA

Commercial Laundry Service

Some organizations and institutions choose to contract with a commercial laundry. Commercial contracts can be very effective and time–saving and are appropriate for certain programs, however, most athletic departments, as well as many sports' and fitness clubs, are limited financially and perceive this as an area in which to save money. Normally, the larger the quantity of laundry, the greater the potential for saving by doing laundry in-house. Lizarraga (1989, p. 66) suggests that outside services cost one–third to one–half more than on–premise laundries.

Another disadvantage of the commercial service is that it may not always be available. Regular pick–up and delivery service is not usually available for sports' teams who play weekend and evening games or for fitness clubs that may be open extensive hours.

A third disadvantage to commercial service is security. As mentioned, sports equipment is in great demand among fans and collectors. When uniforms or equipment leave the premises, it is easy to lose track of them and they may be lost or stolen. "When outfitting a player who is close to 7 feet tall, a replacement can't be easily found off the rack," relates Tom Hoffer, Milwaukee Bucks' Team Services/Equipment Manager (cited in Floyd, 1989, p. 48).

Coin–operated Laundries

Some programs have neither in–house laundries nor choose to use a commercial service, but use local coin–operated laundries. This is not ideal, is not time-effective, and will not "ensure the maximum life of athletic uniforms and equipment" ("Save bundles," 1988, p. 62). Hoffer "adds that security was a special concern at neighborhood coin laundries, where fans often wanted a souvenir uniform for their own closet" (cited in Floyd, 1989, p. 48).

In–house Laundry

If the decision is made to launder on the premises, then the laundry area must have adequate space. Because it will be a humid area, the walls and ceilings should be impervious to moisture and must absorb sound (Lizarraga's study, cited in "Save bundles," 1988).

The laundry area should be in or adjacent to the equipment room and close to the distribution area for accessibility, control, and security. Emling (cited in "Wash costs," p. 3) recommends that "one 35- or 50-pound washer-extractor with a compatible tumbler—a 50- or 70-pound dryer—will take care of a school with around 1,000 students" (Figure 5–29).

In addition to space for the washer and dryer, there should be a table for sorting and folding, shelves for supplies, and hanging racks or rods for air-drying items. Laundry carts provide portage of dirty clothing from the issue area to the wash area (Figure 5–30). Lizarraga (1989, October, p. 68) advises that the physical layout of the laundry area "have a work flow pattern that flows from sort, wash, dry and fold toward the storage or distribution area."

FIGURE 5–29 ■ Equipment laundry area.

FIGURE 5–30 ■ Laundry carts provide portage of dirty clothing.

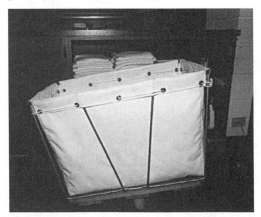

The noise factor should be considered when determining the placement of the laundry room. Donaldson (cited in "Save bundles," 1988, p. 62) recommends locating the laundry on an outside wall for proper dryer venting. "Allow at least 2 feet behind the back of equipment and the wall for service access," says Lizarraga. "Washer–extractors need about 18 inches between them if supply injectors are mounted on the side, while dryers require only about an inch between them" (cited in "Save bundles," 1988, p. 62).

There are laundry systems made especially for athletic departments that feature lower temperature controls and specify that the water should not be over 100 degrees Fahrenheit to prevent fraying and shredding of uniforms ("Save bundles," 1988, April). McArthur's (1990, April) recommendation for drying towels is at 180 to 190 degrees Fahrenheit. Uniforms should be dried at a setting of 145 to 160 degrees Fahrenheit ("How to," 1983, May). Remember that overdrying contributes to the breakdown of garments more than any other factor" (Sain, 1990, September, p. 13).

Other things to remember include: remove items from the dryer immediately to prevent wrinkles; do not overload washers and dryers so they will work well and last longer; remove stains and heavy dirt or other marks before washing; separate garments of different colors; never store items before they are totally dry; always follow the manufacturer's recommendations; and use the correct amount of detergent.

REPAIR AREA

A separate room or space in the equipment room should be provided as a repair area. The area needs to have shelving, cabinet space for repair supplies, a workbench with vise, a sink, a large table, and places to store repair equipment (sewing machines, saws, drills) (Figures 5–31 and 5–32). The ideal repair table is movable with built–in shelves and drawers for hand tools and supplies.

Items to be fixed or reconditioned should be immediately removed from stock and put in the repair area in a predetermined place. Equipment should be fixed as soon as possible so the repair room does not become cluttered. Also, if equipment needing only slight repairs is not repaired immediately, the continued use makes the repair greater and sometimes more costly. The old adage applies to equipment: "a stitch in time saves nine."

The equipment manager should create a schedule for checking all equipment at regular intervals. Protective equipment must be checked frequently. These equipment evaluations should be documented either in handwritten or computer records. This is extremely important for legal purposes; a valid record protects all parties from liability in case of a serious accident.

Annual reconditioning of certain types of equipment, such as football helmets, is required to assure that the equipment is safe and reliable. Riddell Inc., the

FIGURE 5–31 ■ Damaged apparel waiting for repair.

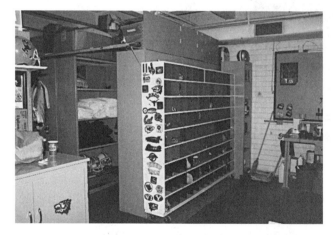

FIGURE 5–32 ■ Designated maintenance area.

nation's largest manufacturer of football helmets, "recently announced that it will no longer recommend reconditioning varsity helmets that are 10 years old or older (or at least 8 years old in the case of youth helmets). Riddell says that helmets over 10 years old should be replaced. Schools that do not follow the manufacturer's recommendations for care and use of its products may risk liability in the event that an athlete is injured" (Pacelli, 1990, p. 15). Bill Hampton, assistant equipment manager of the New York Jets, states, "If the shell is the same, and there's no cracking, there's really no limit on the number of times a set of shoulder pads, or a helmet, or any piece of equipment can be reconditioned. That's the great thing about reconditioning; it's an area in which you can really save money. If I were in charge of a high school program, I'd recondition everything. You can get by for a long time. It costs considerably less to recondition than to replace" (cited from "Buyer's guide," 1989, March, p. 68).

EQUIPMENT MAINTENANCE

Different equipment requires different maintenance. The best recommendation is to follow the manufacturer's instructions, however, a few suggestions are provided in the following list (Ennis, 1983, July).

Archery tackle—lay arrows flat to store and unstring all bows.

Floor mats and bases—repair, clean with soap and water, and store in a dry place. Use rubber or plastic patches to repair outer surfaces.

Inflated balls—slightly deflate balls for storage, but do not flatten. For inflating, moisten the needle with glycerin and insert with a twisting motion. Do not over-inflate. Clean with saddle soap or ball cleaner.

Leather—always dry leather items thoroughly at room temperature and store in a cool, dry area. Mineral oils may be used on leather to prevent hardening. Use saddle soap for cleaning purposes.

Nets—dry thoroughly and roll for storage. Replace worn cables.

Rubber goods—keep away from heat and sunlight during storage. Clean with soap and water.

Wooden equipment—use spar varnish or linseed oil to protect wood. Store javelins and vaulting poles flat and in a dry area out of the way. (Note: Wooden equipment is mostly obsolete, except for "old stock.")

EQUIPMENT TRANSPORTATION

For local or in–house use, lightweight articles (balls, gloves) can be moved easily in nylon mesh bags and heavier items (bats, racquets, golf clubs) in grocery–type or wire carts. It is extremely difficult for one to carry all the equipment to the tennis court or the softball field in one trip or without acquiring additional assistance. A simple cart can be designed to contain all the equipment for a particular sport and can be rolled to the instructional area for distribution (Penman, 1977). As mentioned, there should be an on–site storage area, if feasible.

When necessary to move equipment long distances, arrangements must be made for fast, secure, and effective transportation to assure that the equipment arrives intact and on time. In some cases, particularly with professional teams, a trucking company or van line is hired to transport the equipment, however, this can be costly and is out–of–range financially for many groups.

Many administrators and coaches choose to have all of the equipment, including the complete uniforms, packed and loaded by the equipment manager and staff to assure everything gets to the destination. Most college football teams choose to transport their equipment in the institution's vans or trucks, which are driven by staff members.

For example, the University of Southern Mississippi requires the equipment manager and eight assistants for approximately six hours to load football equipment and uniforms prior to an away game. The manager has specially designed moveable trunks that contain the game shoes, the jerseys, and so on, for the entire team. They work with a checklist for every away game to ensure that all items are packed. Their preplanning assures that the USM football team is fully equipped for each contest (Figure 5–33).

Some competitors, as well as coaches and equipment managers, have had frightening experiences when it was discovered that an essential article had been left behind. San Francisco 49ers equipment manager Bronco Hinek always makes a final check of the locker room after the players have left. "He packs the forgotten helmet or pads, but lets players sweat out their paramnesia, hoping it will engrave the lesson in their brains" (Barks & Muller, 1989, September, p. 63).

Some groups leave the equipment and uniform packing to the athletes. Obviously, this is easier for some sports (tennis) than for others (football). For example, at the 1985 All–Star Baseball Game, Lou Whitaker, starting second baseman for the Detroit Tigers, forgot his uniform and played "on national TV in borrowed pants and cleats and a Tiger jersey, complete with taped–on number, that was hastily purchased at the stadium souvenir shop" (Barks & Muller, 1989, September, p. 63). Regardless of the sport, the transporting of equipment and uniforms is indeed an immense responsibility.

FIGURE 5–33 ■ **Equipment unpacked and in place, ready for the athletes.**

FIGURE 5–34 ■ Electronic controls for temperature and humidity.

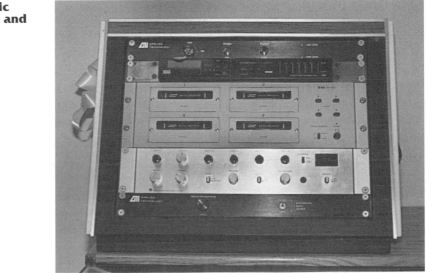

ENVIRONMENTAL AREA CONTROLS

Environmental factors, such as temperature and humidity, are of great concern to the equipment manager. Because the stock needs to be protected from extreme temperature elements and from possible damage by rodents and moths or other insects, the storage area must be well–ventilated, tightly sealed, and contain controls to adjust the levels of humidity and temperature (Jensen, 1983). These controls should be separate from controls for other rooms in the facility. Adequate ventilation is extremely important in storage areas to prevent articles from staleness and mildew. The temperature should range between 60–80 degrees Fahrenheit (Brown, 1989, January). Figure 5–34 shows electronic controls for temperature and humidity.

SUMMARY

Developing and maintaining an efficient storeroom management system is one of the major tasks of the equipment manager. A well-organized and managed equipment room is a reflection of the overall program. Because equipment is a large financial investment for any sports organization, it is imperative to procure the longest life possible for whatever those monies provide.

This chapter discusses the general policies involved in storage and storeroom management, the responsibilities of the equipment manager and staff, equipment room design and space requirements, storage units and other types of storage, laundry and repair areas, equipment maintenance, equipment transportation, and environmental controls for the equipment room.

SELECTED READINGS

American Entrepreneurs Association. (1980). *Physical fitness center* (AEA Business Manual No. 172). Los Angeles: American Entrepreneurs Association.

The Athletic Institute and American Association for Health, Physical Education, and Recreation. (1968). *College and university facilities guide for health, physical education, recreation, and athletics.* Washington, D. C.

Barks, J., & Muller, E. J. (1989, September). Getting in gear. *Sports Travel,* pp. 63–65.

Boevers, G. (1989, August). A clean operation. *College Athletic Management,* pp. 10–13.

Bronzan, R. T. (1974). *New concepts in planning and funding athletic, physical education and recreation facilities,* pp. 105–109, 127–130, 227. St. Paul: Phoenix Intermedia.

Brown, S. D. (1989, January) Stock options. *College Athletic Management,* pp. 19–20.

Buyer's guide to football equipment: taking it from the top. (1989, March). *Scholastic Coach,* pp. 66–69.

Craig, C. (1989, May). Grasping footballs. *College Athletic Management,* pp. 14, 16–17.

Dietrich, J., & Waggoner, S. (1983). *The complete health club handbook.* New York: Simon & Schuster.

Ennis, L. (1983, July). *MWR maintenance management program aid—Care and maintenance of sports equipment,* pp. 1–7. (Available from the Department of the Air Force—Morale, Welfare, & Recreation Center, Arlington, VA 20330-5000).

Evenden, E. S., Strayer, G. D., & Englehardt, N. L. (1938). *Standards for college buildings.* New York City, Teachers College, Columbia University.

Ezersky, E. M., & Theibert, P. R. (1976). *Facilities in sports and physical education.* St. Louis: C. V. Mosby.

Floyd, M. (1989, July). Bucks clean up with new laundry system. *Athletic Business,* pp. 47–48.

Flynn, R. B. (1985). *Planning facilities for athletics, physical education, and recreation,* pp. 39–40, 58, 144–152. North Palm Beach, FL: The Athletic Institute; Reston, VA: American Alliance for Health, Physical Education, Recreation, and Dance.

Fuoss, D. E., & Troppmann, R. J. (1977). *Creative management techniques in interscholastic athletics.* New York: John Wiley.

How to get more years out of your athletic uniforms. (1983, May). *Athletic Purchasing & Facilities,* pp. 24–26, 28–29.

Jensen, C. R. (1988). *Administrative management of physical education and athletic programs,* pp. 352–356. Philadelphia: Lea & Febiger.

Jones, B. J., Wells, L. J., Peters, R. E., & Johnson, D. J. (1988). *Guide to effective coaching— Principles and practice.* Boston, MA: Allyn and Bacon.

Lizarraga, A. (1989, October). Laundry economics. *Athletic Business,* pp. 66–68.

Matthews, D. O. (1987). *Managing collegiate sport clubs.* Champaign: Human Kinetics.

McArthur, S. (1990, April). Towel patrol. *Athletic Business,* pp. 50, 52–53.

Mueller, P., & Reznik, J. W. (1979). *Intramural–recreational sports: Programming and administration.* New York: John Wiley.

National Operating Committee on Standards for Athletic Equipment. *NOCSAE manual.* (Available from the Executive Director, 11724 Plaza Circle, Kansas City, MO 64513)

Pacelli, L. C. (1990, December). Aging helmets to be sidelined. *The Physician and Sports Medicine,* Vol. 18, No. 12, p. 15.

Penman, K. A. (1977). *Planning physical education and athletic facilities in schools,* pp. 261–272. New York: John Wiley.

Sabock, R. J. (1985). *The coach.* Champaign: Human Kinetics.

Sain, T. (1990, September). Practice perfect. *College Athletic Management,* pp. 12–13.

Sapora, A., & Kenney, H. (1961). *A study of the present status. Future needs and recommended standards regarding space used for health, physical education, physical recreation, and athletics.* Champaign: Stipes Publishing.

Save bundles with in–house laundry. (1988, April). *Athletic Business,* pp. 62, 64, 66.

Seefeldt, V. (Ed.). (1987). *Handbook for youth sports coaches.* Reston: National Association of Sport and Physical Education (NASPE) and American Alliance for Health, Physical Education, Recreation, and Dance (AAHPERD).

Stotlar, D. K. (1987). Managing administrative functions with the microcomputer in physical education and sport. In J. E. Donnelly (Ed.), *Using microcomputers in physical education and the sport sciences,* pp. 117–134. Champaign: Human Kinetics.

Thomas, J. R. (Ed.). (1977). *Youth sports guide for coaches and parents.* Manufacturers Life Insurance & National Association for Sport and Physical Education.

Turner, E. T., & McDaniel, C. E. (1990, September). Designing a Teaching/Learning Center. *Journal of Physical Education, Recreation, and Dance,* pp. 20–22.

Walker, M. L. (1989). *A space analysis of physical education activity and ancillary areas in selected small colleges and universities.* Unpublished doctoral dissertation, The University of New Mexico, Albuquerque.

Walker, M. L. (1990, November). [Interview with David Bounds, Equipment Manager, The University of Southern Mississippi, Hattiesburg].

Wash costs down the drain with on–premise laundry. *Athletic Business,* pp. 1–4. (Available from Pellerin Milnor Corporation, P.O. Box 400, Kenner, LA 70063).

Chapter Six

BUDGETING CONCEPTS AND PRINCIPLES

John F. Warner, Assistant Dean, The University of New Mexico

INTRODUCTION

This chapter provides a broad-based overview to concepts and techniques of budgeting, which are useful to any manager, whether in a for-profit or not-for-profit organization.

The chapter begins by discussing the concept of budgeting; then it looks at the purposes of budgeting and at budgeting principles. The major part of the chapter consists of detailed discussion of various types of budgets with specific examples. These are followed by a brief commentary on budgetary control techniques.

THE CONCEPT OF BUDGETING

A budget is a formal quantitative expression of management plans. The process of budgeting is the development of plans for a stated future time period in numerical terms. As such, budgets are statements of anticipated results, either in financial terms (as in revenue and expense and cash budgets) or in nonfinancial terms (as in materials budgets or space budgets).

It is important to note that budgets are used on individual, departmental, and total organizational level. For example, a student may budget in a general way the amount of hours to study for each university class. On a departmental level, the swimming program develops a detailed budget of all anticipated expenses for a period time. On an organizational level, the athletic department at a university takes all of the individual departmental budgets, summarizes those expenses and anticipated revenues, and factors in general and administrative expenses for the entire athletic department. It is easy to see that the concept of budgeting is useful at different levels of personal and organizational applications.

By stating plans in terms of numbers and breaking them into parts that parallel the parts of an organization, budgets correlate planning and allow delegation of authority without loss of control. In other words, reducing plans to numbers forces a kind of orderliness that permits the manager to see in a clear and timely fashion what resources will be used by whom and where, and what revenues, expenses, or units of input or output the plans will involve. An organization that adopts formal budgeting usually becomes convinced of its helpfulness and would not consider regressing to nonbudgeting techniques. The benefits of budgeting almost always clearly outweigh the cost and the effort. Some kind of budget program is bound to be useful to any organization, regardless of its size or its uncertainties.

PURPOSES OF BUDGETING

Exhibit 6–1 helps portray the purposes of the budget in the framework of the entire organization. This flowchart indicates that there are several opportunities to use budgets. It is critical that the budgeting process be closely aligned with the

EXHIBIT 6–1 ■ The Budget in Strategic Perspective

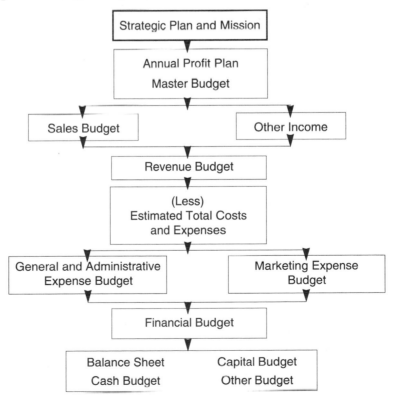

EXHIBIT 6–2 ■ Purposes of Budgeting

- Match income and expenses
- Accomplish objectives
- Plan personnel
- Make purchasing decisions
- Time inflows and outflows
- Delegate authority
- Plan for the future
- Evaluate accomplishments
- Motivate and reward performance

strategic plan and mission. Otherwise, the budgeting process will not accurately reflect the longterm objectives.

The master budget is a yearly operational plan. Sales and income budgets are channelled into the revenue budget, which reflects yearly earnings. Expense budgets follow. Finally, specialized budgets relating to the balance sheet, cash flow, capital purchases, floor space utilization, and so on, can be developed.

Exhibit 6–2 outlines a few of the purposes of budgeting. One primary purpose is to force managers to think ahead—to anticipate and prepare for changing conditions. This planning and budgeting process allows the organization to match income and expenses for future periods of time. It forces the organization to list the objectives that it would like to accomplish. In so doing, the organization and management must look at alternative strategies to meet these objectives. Such objectives might be enunciated in the form of personnel planning—what sort of expertise do we need in the future? The budgeting process also highlights purchasing decisions, when they must be made, and details of timeliness and costliness. Budgeting allows the manager to look at the question of timeliness not only of inflows and outflows of revenues, but also of inflows and outflows of materials, equipment, and cash. The budgeting process allows a manager to delegate to appropriate individuals some responsibility and authority at different levels of the organization. In turn, the manager can evaluate accomplishments of programs, departments, and individuals. Indeed, budgeting can be an effective tool for motivating greater employee productivity and rewarding exemplary performance.

One of the most important purposes of budgeting is to facilitate communication at all levels of the organization. It obliges managers to discuss continually and evaluate reality as compared to the plan (the budget). This sparks discussion regarding the eternal question, "How are we doing?" The budget is effective as a mechanism to control and allocate resources only when it is revised, discussed, and integrated with the strategic plan.

Exhibit 6–3 ■ The Budgeting Process

1. Clarifying purpose of budget
2. Collecting budget information
3. Drafting the budget
4. Adopting the budget
5. Exchanging budget information
6. Evaluating the budget

THE BUDGETING PROCESS

The budgeting process is often imprecise, because it involves a variety of people and perspectives. Exhibit 6–3 gives an outline of this process, which typically occurs in the sequence listed. The manager in charge of a unit or department is responsible for this process.

The first step is to make certain that everyone involved understands what the budget process should accomplish. Often, organizations rush into budgeting without giving this any thought. Therefore, it is important to think about the purpose of developing a budget process. Before going further, it is crucial to answer such questions as, "What should the budget measure?", "How will it be measured?", "By whom?", "Who is responsible for seeing that the budget is carried out?", and so forth.

The next step is to collect appropriate budget information. This stage may involve several participants in the organization or department. It is important for the manager to remember that having many people participate in the information gathering process is valuable. Not only will many of these people have more accurate information than the manager, but their involvement may increase their commitment to making the budget process successful.

The next two steps are drafting the budget and adopting the budget. Usually one person is responsible for authoring the budget, or writing it in specific terms. This written budget is then proposed to the appropriate authorities who decide whether or not to adopt it.

The next step is determining who will receive budget information and how to convey it. It is critical that the appropriate individuals receive budget information on a timely basis. The last step of the budget process is the evaluation. The primary purpose of the evaluation step is to compare actual performance to planned or budgeted performance. By doing this, the manager can see if revisions are necessary and can also use this information for planning and control purposes.

EXHIBIT 6–4 ■ Types of Budgets Used in Equipment Management

1. Equipment budget
2. Revenue and expense budget
3. Labor budget
4. Cash budget
5. Capital expenditure budget
6. Space budget

TYPES OF BUDGETS

There are many types of budgets, which can be classified into several basic types as shown in Exhibit 6–4. A budget summary portrays all of an organization's budgets. As such, it represents the compilation and integration of the individual budgets mentioned in Exhibit 6-4, which is not an exhaustive list. A manager or organization can create a budget for virtually any segment of its operation. The six types of budgets listed in Exhibit 6–4 represent those used most frequently in organizations that deal with the management of equipment.

The Equipment Budget

Exhibit 6–5 is an equipment budget. This example projects the equipment expenses for a men's swimming program at Anyplace University, for the period of one fiscal year. Many budgets, however, take into consideration shorter increments of time. For example, many organizations budget on a monthly, quarterly, or semiannual basis.

The equipment list in Exhibit 6–5 is by no means exhaustive, but indicates how an equipment budget might unfold by concept. When the list of required

EXHIBIT 6–5 ■ Equipment Budget

Anyplace University
Men's Swimming
Jan. 1, 1994–Dec. 31, 1994

Equipment item	
swim trunks (50 @ $10)	$ 500
warm-ups (20 @ $50)	1000
goggles (60 @ $5)	300
kickboards (20 @ $20)	400
fins (20 @ $15)	300
weight room (prorated share of university wt. rm.)	2000
TOTAL equipment expense	**$4500**

items is complete, the quantity and cost for each item is figured. For example, 50 pairs of swim trunks at $10 each will cost $500. The first five equipment items are budgeted the same way, quantity times unit cost. The entry for the weight room, however, is one round figure for use of the university weight room on a prorated basis, perhaps determined by percentage of use. Whatever method determines the $2000 charge for the men's swimming team to use the weight room at the university facility, it must be incorporated in the budget for the entire men's swimming program and must be clear to those approving and implementing the budget.

Total equipment expense for men's swimming for the fiscal year 1994 is anticipated to be $4,500. However, this total expense does not reveal the detail that goes into producing a budget like this. For example, how was the $10 per pair of swim trunks and $50 per warm-up determined? Purchasing guidelines at Anyplace University dictate how the men's swimming program can buy these items, through a competitive bidding or noncompetitive bidding process or by direct purchase. Organizations usually have a spending limit, below which noncompetitive bidding might apply. If Anyplace University had a limit of $500, then before the swimming program could purchase its warm-ups and swim trunks, it would have to receive competitive bids from eligible vendors. This would mean drafting several proposed budgets based on various costs for each item that must be purchased by selection from bids.

The Revenue and Expense Budget

The most frequently used budget spells out plans for revenues and operating expenditures in terms of dollars. Exhibit 6–6 is a basic example of a revenue and expenditure budget, representing projected revenues and expenditures for Betsy's Health Club for the calendar year 1994. The first revenue listed is membership fees, projected at $60,000 over the course of the year. A monthly membership fee projection might be useful in arriving at the entire year's projected sales. Membership fees in a health club are essentially a forecast of sales. Many organizations would spend a significant amount of time trying to forecast sales. In fact, a sales budget would be very useful in describing in detail how the health club arrived at $60,000 in sales for the entire year.

Sales forecasting usually combines various techniques, including seeking opinions of the sales staff, statistical methods, correlating history of sales and economic indicators, gathering opinions of line management, and pricing policies. Each of these has a significant effect on sales forecasting.

Betsy's Health Club also forecasts sales of equipment and retail items, which includes swimming gear, racquetballs, and other equipment or clothing that is sold directly at the health club. Forecasts are also developed for food and beverages, anticipating $8,000 revenue. The final revenue category is "other income,"

EXHIBIT 6–6 ■ **Revenue and Expense Budget**

Betsy's Health Club
Jan. 1, 1994–Dec. 31, 1994

Revenues		
Membership fees (300 @ $200)	$60,000	
Equipment and retail sales		
(swim gear, racquetballs, etc.)	12,000	
Food and beverage sales	8,000	
Other income	5,000	
Total Revenue	**$85,000**	
Expenses		
Salaries	$60,000	
Merchandise	6,000	
Food and beverages	5,000	
Misc. supplies	2,000	
Advertising and marketing	3,000	
Other expenses (utilities, taxes, insurance)	7,000	
Total Expenses	**$83,000**	
Net Income (or loss)	**2,000**	

which might include interest income, income on other investments, or nonrecurring items that are not a major part of the revenue stream of the health club. Total revenues are $85,000.

The major expense is salaries, which are itemized in Exhibit 6–7. Merchandise expenses of $6,000, food and beverage expenses of $5,000, and advertising and marketing expenses of $3,000, make up a significant part of the expense budget. Miscellaneous supplies of $2,000 would include such things as office supplies.

EXHIBIT 6–7 ■ **Labor Budget**

Betsy's Health Club
Jan. 1, 1994–Dec. 31, 1994

Wages and Salaries	
Director	$25,000
Asst. Director/Health Consultant (P/T)	10,000
Exercise instructors (500 hrs. @ $10/hr.)	5,000
Receptionist	10,000
Sales clerk	8,000
Bookkeeper (P/T)	2,000
Total wages and salaries	**$60,000**

Other expenses would include such items as utilities, transportation, interest expense, and taxes. Each item under the subheading of other expenses could be projected in greater detail, depending on the needs of the manager and the organization.

Total expenses equal $83,000, leaving a net income, or profit, for 1994 of $2,000. Generally, revenues and expenses are listed in budget format in the order of their magnitude as well as the significance of their occurrence within the organization.

The Labor Budget

As mentioned, Exhibit 6–7 describes in detail the wages and salaries that Betsy's Health Club anticipates paying during the year 1994. The director's salary will be $25,000 and a part-time assistant director and health consultant will be paid $10,000. A team of exercise instructors (aerobics, swimming, weight room) will be paid $5,000 for 500 hours of instruction at $10 per hour. A receptionist will be paid $10,000, a sales clerk $8,000, and a part-time bookkeeper $2,000. This means that the health club will pay total wages and salaries of $60,000 during 1994, which is the top line item of expenses in the revenue and expense budget (see Exhibit 6–6).

In determining the labor budget, it is important to remember that not only must direct wages and salaries be included but also the appropriate fringe benefits. Exhibit 6–7 does not account for fringe benefits yet the manager must look at recent legislation that is law (such as worker's compensation, minimum wage laws, and social security laws). Many organizations neglect to look at the fringe benefit expenses related to salaries. In many organizations these fringe benefit expenses can exceed thirty percent of actual wage and salary figures.

The Cash Budget

Exhibit 6–8 is the cash budget for Betsy's Health Club for the three-month period of January through March, 1994. A cash budget is usually done on a monthly basis because of short-term cash needs that many businesses have. While Exhibit 6–8 shows the first three months of 1994 (one quarter), a cash budget for the year would list similar line items on a monthly basis through December, 1994.

The cash budget should not be confused with budgeting revenues (see Exhibit 6–6). The cash budget deals only with cash (inflows and outflows over a period of time) where a revenue budget includes sales that are made on account or credit card. The cash budget is perhaps the most critical in determining the viability of a business on a month-to-month basis. If a business runs out of cash, it must find alternative sources of funds to pay its bills.

EXHIBIT 6–8 ■ Cash Budget

Betsy's Health Club
January, 1994–March, 1994

	Jan.	Feb.	Mar.
Beginning monthly balance	$2,000	2,000	2,000
Add: membership fee	3,000	5,000	6,000
retail sales	1,000	1,000	1,500
food sales	500	500	1,000
interest income	0	0	0
Cash available for use	6,500	8,500	10,500
Deduct:			
payroll	3,000	5,000	5,000
merchandise	1,500	0	500
food	500	300	600
utilities	300	300	500
interest	0	0	0
taxes	0	0	200
other expenses	700	300	400
Preliminary balance	500	2,600	3,300
Minimum required cash balance	2,000	2,000	2,000
Excess (or deficiency)	(1,500)	600	1,300
Short-term investment of excess			400
Liquidation of short-term investment			
Short-term loan to cover deficiency	1,500		
Repayment of short-term loan		600	900
Ending monthly balance	$2,000	$2,000	$2,000

The starting point for determining a cash budget is deciding the minimum cash balance "cushion," that a firm needs at all times. For Betsy's Health Club it is $2,000. The minimum balance allows cash for the daily transactions that occur in a normal business. This minimum cash balance is the top line of the budget—the beginning monthly balance.

The next step is to project all of the cash inflows anticipated during the month. For Betsy's Health Club this includes membership fees of $3,000, retail sales of $1,000, food sales of $500 for a total cash available figure of $6,500. Next, cash outflows are projected. These outflows include payroll expenses of $4,000, merchandise purchases of $1,500, food purchases of $500, utilities expenses of $300, and other expenses of $700 during January. A preliminary balance of $500 indicates that cash inflows exceed cash outflows by that amount, but because the minimum required cash balance is $2,000, there is a deficit of $1,500. This deficiency can be overcome through a short-term loan. The loan of $1,500 plus the cash inflow of $500 leaves the ending monthly balance of $2,000.

The same process is then used for February and March and subsequent months. That is to say, the ending balance for one month becomes the beginning balance for the following month. Cash inflows and outflows are again projected on a monthly basis.

In the month of February, an excess cash flow of $600 is projected and used to pay part of the $1,500 loan taken in January. For the month of March an excess of $1,300 is projected, $900 of which will pay the balance of the short-term loan, while $400 will be invested. Short-term investment opportunities allow a business to turn excess cash into greater profits without seriously debilitating their cash flow.

Other Budgets

The capital expenditure budget (see Exhibit 6–4) outlines specific capital expenditures for machinery, equipment, inventories, and other items. Whether for a short period or a long one, these budgets require care because they give definite shape to plans for spending the funds of a business. Capital expenditure budgets are usually tied in with fairly long-range planning, because many purchases of equipment and other capital items are not made frequently.

The space budget (see Exhibit 6–4) is a good example of a budget that is better expressed in quantities rather than monetary terms. The dimension of expression for most space budgets is number of square feet allocated. For example, at Betsy's Health Club a space budget might determine how much space (in square feet) to allocate for food and beverage sales, merchandise sales, a swimming pool, an exercise room, a weight room, and so on. Space budgets are useful especially in dealing with questions of remodeling and reallocating physical space as demands of customers and the marketplace change.

It might be useful to an organization and its manager(s) to budget many other items. Examples are a sales budget, machine hours of expensive exercise equipment, units of materials used, advertising, and so on. It is important to budget (income and expenses) for all areas that have a significant impact on business.

BUDGETARY CONTROL

When budgetary controls are effective, it is partly because managers know that budgets are only tools that assist but do not replace good management. Budgets have limitations and must be tailored to each job. Moreover, they are the tools of all managers and not only of the budget director. One of the keys to successful budgeting is to develop and make available standards by which programs and work can be translated into specific needs for labor, operating expenses, space, and other resources. Managers should compare actual and forecasted performance in their areas. This information must be designed to show them how well they are doing. Unfortunately, such information is usually not available until it is too late for the manager to avoid budget mistakes.

Because dangers arise from inflexibility in budgets and because maximum flexibility consistent with efficiency underlines good planning, attention has been increasingly given to variable budgets. These are designed to vary according to variations in the volume of sales, or some other measure of output. Variable budgets can show how expense items change as sales volume changes. The big advantage with flex-variable budgeting is that it creates a contingency approach to budgeting and planning. It allows the manager to look at different expense configurations as sales volumes increase or decrease. In fact, many organizations prepare several budgets to look at a variety of sales volumes. In this fashion, they are best prepared for deviations that might be dictated by their customers and the marketplace.

Another type of budgeting is called *zero-based budgeting*. The idea behind this technique is to divide enterprise programs into subunits composed of goals, activities, and needed resources. Then costs are calculated for each package from the ground up. By starting the budget of each package from base zero, costs are calculated afresh for each budget period, thus avoiding the common tendency in budgeting to look only at changes from a previous period. This technique is most frequently applied to support areas, such as personnel, on the assumption that there is some room for discretion in these areas.

It is important to note some cautions and dangers in the budgeting process. The first caution has to do with philosophy. Should budget figures be set in a conservative fashion in order to stay within achieved boundaries? Or should budgets be set in a more aggressive fashion in order to "stretch" the organization? Neither of these extremes is beneficial. The budgeting process should incorporate realistic projections.

Another danger with regard to budgeting is spelling out minor expenses or revenues in too much detail, thereby depriving managers of needed freedom. Too much detail in the budget process can become cumbersome. After all, the manager is there to enhance revenues or control expenses, not to fill out or review too much budgeting paperwork! Another caution lies in allowing budget goals to become more important than company goals. In their zeal to keep within budget limits, managers may focus on dollars and cents but forget the company mission and goals.

Another danger is that budgeting may be used to hide inefficiencies. Budgets have a way of growing from precedent—the fact that a certain expenditure was made in the past can become evidence for its reasonableness in the present. This is one of the reasons zero-based budgeting has become so popular. It requires managers to justify each expense from zero dollars for future periods of time. Just because an expense was appropriate last year does not mean that it will be appropriate in coming years.

Finally, budgets are not cast in concrete. This is one of the advantages of variable budgets. They allow for changing budgets in midstream. If circumstances dictate, budgets should and must be revised. The budget should not become a ball and chain around the leg of the manager.

OTHER CONSIDERATIONS

The personal computer (PC) has direct application to the budgeting process. The PC increasingly appeals to managers because it is flexible and relatively inexpensive and can be used more quickly than a manual budgeting system. Some budgeting applications for the personal computer deal with the whole process of budget preparation, graphic presentation, electronic spreadsheets, word processing, forecasting, and financial analysis. Many of these PC applications can be enhanced through a sophisticated array of appropriate software. Because the technology for the PC changes so rapidly, it is important for the manager to develop an understanding of available software before generating a manual budget system.

SUMMARY

The budget is a management tool. It will not increase sales nor reduce expenses by itself. This requires management, decision making, and analysis. In order for the budgeting process to be effective, budgets should be prepared on a timely basis. That is, they should be done well in advance of the beginning of the fiscal year. Budget information needs to flow to the appropriate individuals on a timely basis so that they can make changes as appropriate. Only by following these and other principles mentioned throughout this chapter will the budget and budgeting process be an effective management tool.

SELECTED READINGS

Anthony, et al. (1991). *Management control systems* (7th ed.). Chicago: Irwin.

Duffy, M. (1989, January/February). ZBB, MBO, PPB, and their effectiveness within the planning/marketing process. *Strategic Management Journal,* pp. 163–173.

Garrison, R. (1991). *Managerial accounting* (6th ed.). Chicago: Irwin.

Horngren, C. (1990). *Introduction to management accounting* (7th ed.). Englewood Cliffs, NJ: Prentice Hall.

Shelton, F., & Bates, J. (1986, July). How to create an electronic spreadsheet budget. *Management accounting,* (7th ed.). Englewood Cliffs, NJ: Prentice Hall.

Umapathy, S. (1987, February). How successful firms budget. *Management accounting,* pp. 25–27.

Chapter Seven

LEGAL LIABILITY AND SAFETY FACTORS

C. Newton Wilkes, Human Performance and Recreation,
The University of Southern Mississippi

INTRODUCTION

Much has been written relative to the legal implications connected with sports and related professions. Legal framework includes parameters for sports participants, sports management (from officials to coaches), sports spectators, sports facilities, sports equipment, and product liability.

A recent trend throughout the United States is the willingness of the public to sue in the event of an injury or civil problem. This trend is magnified when one considers the vast amount of monetary awards acquired through litigation (Horine, 1991).

In many instances, individuals seem to pursue legal action just to test laws and/or possibly sympathetic jurors. It is wise for every person working in sports

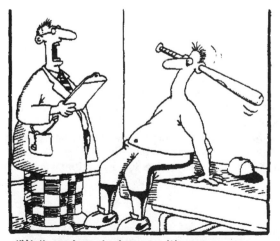

"Well, you're a lucky man, it's not a career-ending injury. Of course, you'll have to be careful walking through doorways.

facilities and with sports equipment to be aware of legal responsibilities and to perform all consumer services with these in mind.

There are a myriad of circumstances by which the most well-intentioned professional can become involved in litigation. What must be done, then, is to conduct programs in a safe, healthy, and prudently administered environment. Health and safety of participants should never be compromised or sacrificed.

This chapter provides an overview of legal implications, a reflection of legal liability, and some safety considerations. In-depth treatment of every legal situation is not possible, however, some practical and pertinent information provides guidelines and insights in areas of particular concern to sports professionals.

LEGAL TERMS AND DEFINITIONS

When dealing with legalities, it is valuable to understand terminology. The following is a list of frequently used terms. Before taking legal action, one should consult an attorney (preferably a sports attorney) licensed in the specific area of litigation to ensure full protection according to the laws of that state.

Act of God—an unavoidable accident that occurs through the fault of no human being, but because of some circumstance in nature, such as tornadoes, hail, floods, and lightning. If negligence was not a factor, an award might be based on some other legal factor.

Agreement to participate—a consent form, a signed statement (not a contract) that involves an assumption of risk on the part of the participant; parents/guardian and participant consent that they understand the inherent dangers, including injury and death, and know the importance of following rules and instruction.

Assumption of risk—a doctrine suggesting that in certain sports, games, or environment, an inherent risk to the participant is noted. The participant is aware of the risk and voluntarily exposes himself or herself to the dangers and conditions for potential injury.

Attractive nuisance—a facility, piece of equipment, or other object that, by its very nature, tends to attract trespassers, who may cause themselves damage by use.

Comparative and contributory negligence—a prorated comparison of the negligence contributed by both parties involved in an injury; the comparative/contributory negligence is usually expressed in percentages attributed to the plaintiff and defendant.

Damages—compensation, usually monetary, awarded to an individual injured because of action or inaction by another individual; the award may be based on actual and/or punitive damages.

Defendant—one who is accused of causing an injury through some perceived or real negligence; one who denies a claim.

Disclaimer—a repudiation or denial of responsibility, usually for potential injury to participants, which is clearly stated prior to the activity.

Discrimination—the showing of favoritism or noting differences in the treatment of others; partiality exhibited because of differences; unequal treatment.

Due process—the right to be heard, to defend against claims, to appeal, to receive fair and equal treatment, according to the law.

Exculpatory agreement—an agreement between parties, where one of the parties to the agreement excuses or justifies the other party from alleged fault or guilt.

Foreseeability—the ability to see or know in advance; the reasonable anticipation that harm or injury is a likely result of acts or omissions.

Governmental function—the functions of an entity, state, municipality, and such, which are essential to its existence and which tend to serve the public at large; activities carried on by a governmental body, pursuant to state requirement and the discharge of its obligation for health, safety, or general welfare of the public at large.

Indemnification—protecting employees and agencies from compensatory losses in the event of a judgement against an agency; a guarantee to make restitution for damages; protection in the form of liability insurance for employees or agencies using the host agency's facilities.

In loco parentis—acting in place of the parent or guardian in behalf of the child.

Judgment—on a claim in which a person believes there is no genuine issue of material fact and that he or she is entitled to prevail as a matter of law.

Liability—the condition, state, or obligation to do a particular thing and for which an individual or agency is legally responsible; legal obligation to act prudently.

Litigation—a lawsuit contested in a court of law for person enforcing a right or seeking a remedy.

Negligence—conduct that falls below standards established by law to protect others from harm or unreasonable risks; failure to act as a reasonably prudent individual either by commission or omission of action.

Plaintiff—one who is injured; the party complaining or bringing suit against another.

Product liability—legal responsibility to manufacture and place on the market equipment and supplies that are safe in design and in purpose of their use; if defective, litigation may ensue.

Proprietary function—discretionary functions of an entity, state, city, or municipality which are considered to be in the best interest of the members of said entity or citizens of said state or municipality; those functions exercised for the peculiar benefit and advantage of the members or citizens of the entity or state; as opposed to functions and official duties to the citizenry at large.

Proximate cause—reasonably or sufficiently close causal connection between the conduct of the agency or individual and the resulting injury or loss to another.

Prudent person—one who acts in a reasonable, careful, discreet, and judicious manner.

Punitive damages—monetary award intended to punish wrongdoer; usually awarded in addition to actual damages.

Tort—twisted or wrong; a civil wrong (not involving a breach of contract) that produces an injury or loss to another person or property.

Waiver—conscious and voluntary surrender of a known right; a signed statement that an individual will not hold the agency responsible for accidents that may occur; becomes invalid in the case of children who cannot legally sign away their right to sue.

GENERAL LIABILITY FACTORS

In the past, many of the state agencies within the fifty United States relied on governmental immunity to exclude them from litigation, whether or not negligence could be attributed to that governmental agency. According to Appenzeller (1980), there is a trend away from the governmental immunity doctrine and, because of an informed public, more court cases are being pursued on the basis that negligence has become a primary factor to test the legal realm of the court system. This seems particularly true since there is a trend among the states toward the recognition of proprietary (permissive) functions rather than mandatory functions of government (health, education, and welfare of citizens).

Consequently, interscholastic and intercollegiate coaches and administrators of athletic programs, fitness managers, physical educators, recreation personnel, and the like, need to understand and adhere to sound, prudent practices, and principles for all participants under their supervision. The following cases serve as examples.

[Dibortolo v. Metropolitan School District of Washington Township, 440 N.E. 2d. Court of Appeals of Indiana, 2nd District, 506, October 7, 1982]

Facts: The plaintiff, Mary Ann Dibortolo, brought a negligence suit against the Metropolitan School District for injuries that she sustained during a physical education class. On March 15, 1977, Mary was an eleven-year-old sixth-grade student. She broke a tooth while performing an exercise called the vertical jump. She lost her balance and fell into the wall. The teacher said that she always considered safety aspects. She said that she never let the kids jump near the wall, but other students testified otherwise.

Issue: Did the teacher demonstrate correctly the exercise before she allowed the students to perform it?

Decision: The court found in favor of the plaintiff because in this case the evidence proved that the teacher was negligent when she did not demonstrate the exercise. Due to this lack of instruction, a proximate cause of the plaintiff's injury is one that sets in motion the chain of circumstances leading to the injury.

[Kain v. Rockridge Community Unit School District No. 300, 453 N.E. 2d Appellate Court of Illinois, 3rd District, 118, August 26, 1983]

Facts: Kain, a student, brought suit against school district, teacher, and football coach, seeking compensation for injuries sustained in a high school football game. The plaintiff alleged negligence by the coach for allowing him to play in a game prior to meeting the number of practices required by Illinois High School Association (IHSA).

Issue: Do Illinois statutes, which grant teachers and school districts immunity from negligence, apply to coaches who allegedly violated IHSA rules concerning practice requirements prior to playing in a game?

Decision: The Circuit Court, Fourteenth Judicial Court, Rock Island County, granted the defendants' motion to dismiss the complaint based on statutory immunity, and the plaintiff appealed. The Third District Appellate Court of Illinois ruled the following: (1) the defendants were acting in loco parentis and, under statute, were not liable for mere negligence, (2) the statute that confers immunity on teachers and school districts from negligence in the supervision of activities connected with school districts and the coach allegedly violated an Illinois High School Association rule prohibiting students from playing football without adequate practice. While the plaintiff argued that the rule is a prohibition leaving the teacher no discretion and that the statute was thus inapplicable, the statute, which speaks only of supervision, does not just apply to situations in which a teacher has discretion.

[Akins v. Glens Falls City School District, 424 N.E. 2d. Court of Appeals of New York, 531, June 18, 1981]

Facts: A spectator at a high school baseball game was struck by a foul ball while standing along the third base line. The school district had in place a 24' high x 50' wide screen behind the home plate area. The spectator was not assigned a specific area from which to watch the game by the school district, and seating was still available behind the screened area.

Issues: (1) Did the school district provide reasonable care in its installation of the screened area? (2) Was there adequate seating in the screened area? and (3) Did the school district create a breach of duty by not extending the screened area?

Decision: Warren County Supreme Court ruled in favor of the plaintiff in a jury trial. The defendant appealed and the case went to the New York Court of Appeals. The Court of Appeals ruled that the school district needed to provide protection only in the home plate area. Because a screen was in place and adequate seating was available, the school district was not liable for failing to provide additional protection. The field owner is only under duty to exercise reasonable care under the circumstances to prevent injury to spectators. The Appeals Court overturned the lower court ruling and dismissed the complaint.

Broad implications arise from the fact that, according to Bucher (1987, p. 341), "approximately 65% to 70% of all jurisdiction accidents involving boys and 59% to 65% involving girls occur in physical education and recreation programs." These data become magnified when one considers that there are approximately 20 million youngsters participating in youth sports each year (Seefeldt, 1987). Of import, also startling, is the fact that "physical educators are involved in more than 50% of the injuries sustained by students each year" (Bucher, 1987, p. 340).

What, then, are the general liability factors apparently causing the damages? The primary factors that are mentioned in litigation include: liability; negligence; torts—unintentional, intentional, nuisance; lack of standard of care; improper, inadequate, or lack of supervision; breach of duty; proximate cause; willful and wanton misconduct; foreseeability; failure to act as a prudent person; in loco parentis; discrimination; improper due process; and, comparative/contributory negligence.

The following cases serve as examples of defense for some of the aforementioned terms.

[Hearl v. Waterbury Y.M.C.A. Conn., 444 A 2d. Supreme Court of Connecticut, 211, May 4, 1982]

Facts: Hearl, the plaintiff, was participating in a volleyball game at a facility maintained by the Waterbury Y.M.C.A. The plaintiff sustained permanent and disabling injuries when he made contact with another player. The injuries occurred during the last game of an all-day tournament in which alcoholic beverages had been consumed. There was no direct supervision of tournament by Y.M.C.A. staff. The plaintiff sued the Y.M.C.A. and another player.

Issue: Was there a breach of duty on the part of the defendant which resulted in injury to the plaintiff?

Decision: In an out-of-court settlement the plaintiff and another player reached a $25,000 settlement. The Superior Court of Waterbury set aside the jury verdict on behalf of the plaintiff. On appeal, the Supreme Court of Connecticut held that any failure by the organization to provide supervision of the volleyball game was not a substantial factor in causing the plaintiff's injuries. The plaintiff did not establish a causal connection between his injury and the lack of supervision. Based on this ruling, the organization did not breach its duty and the lower court decision was upheld.

[Thomas v. St. Mary's Roman Catholic Church, 283 N.W. 2d. Supreme Court of South Dakota, 254, September 12, 1979]

Facts: A high school student and his father brought personal injury actions against the church because the student crashed through glass paneling while playing basketball in the church gymnasium. The student, a male, was performing a lay-up. Due to the injuries from the accident the boy lost 25% use of both arms.

Issues: Was the church negligent? Could the church foresee the possibility of injury? Did the boy, by coming into the gym, assume the risk of potential injury?

Decision: The court found in favor of the plaintiff. The church was found negligent because it should have foreseen the glass as a hazard, and the church did not do anything to prevent the possibility of an injury. It might have been a different judgment if the church had installed unbreakable glass. With regard to the question of the plaintiff's assumption of risk, the court said that the charges were null because the boy did not voluntarily assume the risk, because he was not aware of the dangers.

[O'Conner v. Board of Education of School District 23, 545. U.S. District Court, N.D. Illinois, E.D., F. Supp. 376, August 12, 1982]

Fact: The school board and other defendants filed a motion for summary judgement in action brought by an 11-year-old girl and her parents. They were seeking an injunction requiring her to be permitted to try out for the boys' basketball team at her school.

Issue: Since she was seven years old, Karey O'Conner had been playing with boys so she felt that only the boys' basketball team could provide her with a level of competition sufficiently high to enable her to develop her skills. The defendants refused to allow Karen to try out for the boys' team; their policy was to maintain separate basketball teams for boys and girls to maximize the participation of both sexes in interscholastic sports.

Decision: The court ruled that a recipient that operates or sponsors interscholastic, intercollegiate, club, or intramural athletics shall provide equal opportunity for members of both sexes. The Title IX Education Amendment of 1972 requires educational institutions to accommodate interest and abilities for both sexes, which was done. As long as girls' basketball is offered, the girl will not be able to try out for the boys' basketball team.

[Fortin v. Darlington Little League, 514 F. 2d. U.S. Court of Appeals, 1st Circuit Rhode Island, 344, March 31, 1975]

Facts: Allison "Pookie" Fortin was denied participation in the Pawtucket, Rhode Island, Little League. The court ruled that, although Little League is a private organization, there was significant necessary government involvement: Little League diamonds were laid out and maintained by the city according to specifications and for the primary benefit of the Little League, the general public was "often precluded from utilizing the facilities," and because of the interest and involvement of the city and the sympathetic relationship it had with the Little League, a government function was being carried on by a quasi-private organization.

Issue: Answering arguments that girls were weaker and more injury prone than boys, the court responded... "A sex-based classification denies equal protection in the constitutional sense unless shown to rest on a convincing factual rationale going beyond 'archaic and overbroad generalizations' about the different roles of men and women."

Decision: It was determined that girls were discriminated against merely because they were girls and for no apparent significant reason. "All girls were rejected regardless of individual strength and prowess; even those boys who were physically weak, awkward, or disabled found places on teams, a distinct denial of equal protection."

How can school, athletic, fitness, and recreation personnel decrease the probability of a lawsuit? First of all, one should remember that the plaintiff, in order to be awarded restitution for damages, must prove negligence, or some form of it. That, in itself, is more difficult in some instances than in others.

Baley and Matthews (1984) suggest that the public needs to be educated about the inherent risks of athletics and recreational pursuits. The same authors also encouraged continuously striving to reduce the number of injuries, particularly debilitating or fatal injuries. A third way, which they present, to lessen probability of a lawsuit is to maintain accurate, complete records of injuries. Explanatory documentation of drills and techniques used to establish required skills pertinent to a sport are beneficial. In all situations, the health and safety of the participants are paramount and must not be sacrificed. This concerns not only competitive or recreational events, but also equipment and facilities (Horine, 1991).

Increasingly, line litigation or *respondeat superior* negligence cases have surfaced. In simple terms, this means that more than one individual may be sued and follows the chain of command of the defendant's superiors. Several cases involving court action against the teacher/coach, principal, supervisor, the school board, and district superintendent are on record. Ultimately, then, the entire system of individuals may be placed on trial. Because some states continue to recognize sovereign immunity, many plaintiffs initiate court proceedings against individual defendants rather than the state agency.

[Durham v. Forest Preserve District of Cook County, 504 N.E. 2d. Appellate Court of Illinois, 1st District, 899, February 10, 1987]

Facts: A 16-year-old boy skipped school with a classmate and went to Schiller Woods Forest Preserve (Illinois). After drinking some beer, the boy and some friends carried a picnic table to Schiller Pond and threw it in the water to raft. There were "No Swimming" signs posted. During the horseplay on the "raft," one teenager fell into the water and drowned. The boy's mother filed a claim charging the Forest Preserve with willful and wanton misconduct in the operation of the pond. However, the court ruled there was no duty of care owed to her son because the pond presented an open and obvious danger, of which he should have been aware.

Issue: An occupier or owner of land is required to remedy conditions which, though harmless to adults, are dangerous to children, who may foreseeably wander onto the premises. Was this unfortunate result foreseeable?

Decision: The court dismissed the case. If an owner knows or should know that children frequent the premises and if the cause of the child's injury was the dangerous condition, the owner is liable under the terms of ordinary negligence. However, a dangerous condition does not impose a duty on owners to repair the conditions when the risks of danger can be appreciated and avoided by children. Because the boy was of high school age, he was old enough to be allowed at large, and could appreciate the risks presented by Schiller Pond: "Moreover, 'any child of age to be allowed at large,' is expected to appreciate an obvious and open danger." The court examined an Illinois statute that provided a public entity owed a duty of ordinary care to persons whom the entity intended and permitted to use its property. Because the pond was clearly used for fishing, not swimming, and because picnic tables were not intended to be used as rafts, the teenager was not within the class of people intended to use the property. Therefore, no duty of care was owed.

[Gregory P. Neeld, v. American Hockey League, 439 F. Supp. U.S. District Court, W. D. New York, 459, October 25, 1977]

Facts: The American Hockey League (AHL) was denying a hockey player with only one eye the opportunity to play professional hockey. The plaintiff (Gregory Neeld) brought action on claims of violation of the federal civil rights act that states "a person who is partially or totally blind has a constitutional right not to be discriminated against by an employer or prevented from participation in a college sports program because of his or her visual impairment."

Issue: The American Hockey League's constitution had a bylaw stating "a player with one eye, or one of whose eyes has a vision of only 3/60ths or under, shall not be eligible to play for a Member Club."

Decision: This bylaw was ruled unconstitutional. The New York Human Rights Law states that blindness is a disability against which an employer may not discriminate unless sight in one or both eyes is shown to be a bona fide occupational qualification. Because the defendants were unsuccessful in establishing that having sight in both eyes is a bona fide occupational qualification, the court upheld the preliminary injunction against the AHL.

[Ricky Gillespie v. Southern Utah State College v. Scott Brown, M.D.—Third Party, 669 P 2d. Supreme Court of Utah, 861, August 25, 1983]

Fact: Ricky Gillespie, an injured basketball player, sought a malpractice suit against a college and Dr. Brown for negligence that resulted in frostbite of his fourth and fifth toes and smaller areas on the bottom of his foot and heel.

Issue: The question for the jury to decide was whether the tight taping of the injured student's ankle by the trainer in conjunction with ice immersion treatments and failure to elevate the ankle contributed to the student's injuries. There was testimony that the night after the injury Ricky had slept with his ankle submerged in a bucket of ice water.

Decision: The jury returned a verdict in which it found Ricky 100% negligent and such negligence was the proximate cause of his injuries when he fell asleep with his foot in the bucket of ice water. Neither the college nor the trainer was found negligent.

It is generally recognized (Wong, 1988; Frost et al, 1988; Bucher, 1987; Kraus & Curtis, 1982; Horine, 1991) that the plaintiff must prove four specific elements to win a case of negligence: duty owed or standard care and conduct, breach of duty or neglect to conform to standards, proximate cause or actual cause connecting the individual or service to the resulting loss of injury to the plaintiff, and damages and actual loss or injury to the plaintiff.

Even if the plaintiff proves these four factors, the court may lessen the amount of monetary compensation for actual or punitive damages in consideration of elements involving comparative and/or contributory negligence, assumption of risk, attractive nuisance (proper operation, security, supervision, and so on), waiver, disclaimer, act of God, exculpatory agreement, and agreement to participate. In each case, a sharing of the liability or negligence is implied and/or actual. In the majority of litigation, the court decides the ratio or percentage each party is to bear.

PRODUCT LIABILITY—CONSIDERATIONS AND CAUTIONS

"Product liability refers to the liability of a manufacturer, processor, seller, lessor, or anyone furnishing a product that causes injury to another. Liability is predicated on negligence, breach of warranty, or, most recently, strict liability" (Baley and Matthews, 1984, p. 68).

Manufacturers produce a product that is intended for specific purposes. If the consumer purchases the product and uses it in the specific manner for which it is intended, then the product should be safe to use. When a product is defective or is used for unintended purposes, an injury or loss can occur. Injuries and assessments of liability have caused many manufacturers to place warning labels on the product in visible areas. Most indicate that the label is not to be removed nor, as in the case of a football helmet, should the product be tampered with because this may void warranty or displace responsibility to the consumer for altering the product in the event of an injury. Product warning labels should signify potential dangers of a product even if it is used properly and safely (Horine, 1991). Manufacturers of football helmets, diving boards, gymnastics, fitness and exercise equipment have experienced increases in the number of lawsuits. "Manufacturers have pushed for a fault-based standard of liability that would limit their liability to product defects that are clearly the result of manufacturers' negligence, and to the proportion of the blame assigned to the manufacturers" ("Product liability," 1987, January, p. 36). The United States Congress and the Senate, have yet to decide on this action, but the struggle continues.

[Schmitt v. Dudley Sports Co., 279 N.E. 2d. Indiana Court of Appeals, 2nd District, 266, February 22, 1972]

Facts: Danville High School purchased an automatic baseball-pitching machine from Dudley Sports Company. Upon receipt of the machine, the vice principal and the baseball coach uncrated it. The crate contained a parts list, assembly instructions, and a tag warning that the operation of the machine should be understood before uncrating. The tag referred to the operating instructions, but no operating instructions were given. The vice principal and the coach uncrated the machine, assembled it, and used it. It was then placed in the storage room. Schmitt, a student at the school, was severely injured when he was struck by the pitching arm as he swept the room. Schmitt brought an action against the school and Dudley Sports.

Issue: Dudley argued that because a general warning tag was sent to the school, no liability can be attached to Dudley for Schmitt's injuries. Dudley did include a general warning, but it hardly conveyed an implication that the machine would only be dangerous when in operation, and no warning was given of the latent dangers of the machine. Nothing was mentioned about its triggering capabilities when it was unplugged, so a more specific warning was required to fulfill Dudley's duty to harm.

Decision: The jury found from the evidence that Schmitt's injuries were the natural and probable consequence of Dudley's negligence.

According to Howard Bruns, then president of the Sporting Goods Manufacturers Association ("The challenges," 1980, April, p. 12), "not only manufacturers, but school leagues and other sports-related organizations have been hit by increasing insurance costs, litigation, and the threat of litigation to the detriment of their programs and activities." Bruns continues:

The trampoline is virtually non-existent in schools now. The ranks of football helmet manufacturers have been cut in half [more recent data indicate manufacturers have now dwindled from 20 to 2 (Figgue, Rocky Mt. News, October 12, 1988)], yet football-related fatalities are down 55 percent over a 10-year period. It's not the injuries that have brought about the problem but frivolous claims and suits compounded by an over-reaction by the insurance industry in both rate making and settlements of frivolous claims and suits.

[Carrier v. Riddell, Inc. 721 F. 2d U.S. Court of Appeals, 1st Circuit, Massachusetts, 867, November 23, 1983]

Facts: The plaintiff, Mitchell Carrier, suffered a severe spinal injury while participating in a high school football game. He and his mother sued several football helmet manufacturers. They argued that the helmet makers were negligent in failing to warn the team that football helmets do not offer much protection to a player's neck or spine. The Massachusetts District Court ruled in favor of Riddell, Inc., after it was discovered that the injured athlete was not wearing a Riddell helmet. The plaintiffs appealed to the United States Court of Appeals.

Issue: Was there a special reason that the plaintiff required the use of a Riddell helmet which would make Riddell liable because other team members used the Riddell equipment?

Decision: The Appeals Court upheld the lower court decision. The ruling stated that Riddell did not owe the plaintiff any duty of care because the plaintiff was not using its helmet. The ruling stated that there was no tort liability on the part of Riddell. Also, Riddell owed no "duty of care" to someone who did not use its equipment. The court stated that a manufacturer has a duty to warn of the hazards with the use of its products, but is not negligent for users of other manufacturers' products.

Bruns ("The challenges," 1980, April, p. 12) indicates just "how ridiculous and fearful this has become, [as] just recently a class action suit was filed against Atlanta footrace promoters on behalf of several runners because the weather was °too hot during the race." Consequently, product liability has expanded from a product causing injuries to a nonproduct causing related injuries.

An additional liability factor is now used by lawyers and the courts to assess product fault. In cases involving injuries to children, the courts have decided that manufacturers must be cognizant of the term "foreseeability." Swartz (1989, August, pp. 50–53) states that "manufacturers are obligated to design products to reasonably protect children when their contact with the products is foreseeable"... and, in fact, "foresee that a child is likely to use a product without parental supervision and should not manufacture or market a product without regard to this fact."

Stotlar (1987, January, p. 28) agrees, reporting that "manufacturers and purchasers of athletic equipment have in many cases been held to foresee all possible uses and misuses of the equipment and to warn users of the potential risks which accompany the use and misuse of the equipment in question." This has caused a weakening of the defense by assumption of risk (by adults and children) and strengthened the case for "one's voluntary exposure to a known danger" (Stotlar, 1987, p. 28).

Ultimately, the user must be informed of the specific inherent dangers of a product before the user can be held liable. Otherwise, the user cannot be held accountable for all of the assumptions of risks. Manufacturers of a product, on the other hand, can and will be held accountable.

Swartz (1989, August, p. 53), carrying the assumption further, states that, "In many cases, a manufacturer markets a leisure-time product as a toy, rather than as sports equipment, furthering the potential of injury to a child."

RISK MANAGEMENT—RESPONSIBILITY AND PRECAUTIONS

Kaiser (1986, p. 229) states that "the objective of risk management is to efficiently conserve the assets and financial potential resources of the organization and to achieve financial stability by reducing the potential for financial loss." Smart, precise planning, policy making decisions, documentation, and proper use of safety standards for supervision and equipment may help meet this objective.

Risk management has been defined (Horine, 1990, p. 117) as "... more than simply avoiding accidents. It is a total program that analyzes where and why accidents may occur and how the hazards might be controlled, and determines which calculated risks are acceptable." Risk management is not only a plan, it is a defensive yet pro-active stance toward minimizing unsuspecting risk traps. Practitioners beware!

Baron (1988, September, pp. 53–55) lists three factors that may help provide safer facilities: "conduct frequent inspections of equipment and facilities, looking for hazards or potential defects and removing them upon discovery; provide proper supervision during activities; and provide proper warnings on the safe use of the equipment or facility and the inherent dangers of a specific activity (see Figure 7–1).

Further, as Paul Grace reports (1989, March, pp. 20–23), "... the basis of risk management is asking the tough questions and sweating the details."

There is the need then to analyze the risks involved in sports, fitness, and recreational activities, and to make efforts to minimize those risks. Additionally, coaches, teachers, fitness managers, and other related practitioners should under-

Figure 7–1 ■ Signs providing proper rules and warnings are an important part of risk management.

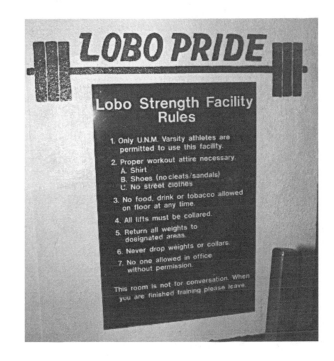

stand their legal duties and responsibilities. Those who provide activities, supervision, facilities, equipment, and care of others within their jurisdiction must act as professionals who perform within a reasonable standard of care, as any prudent individual would act under similar circumstances.

Exhibit 7–1 ■ Legal Duties of Coaches

1. Duty to instruct properly.
2. Duty to warn of the inherent dangers in a sport or other activity.
3. Duty to provide proper supervision.
4. Duty to provide a safe environment.
5. Duty to provide health care (appraisals and follow-up).
6. Duty to enforce rules and regulations.
7. Duty to classify and group participants for competition based upon skill level, age, maturity, sex, size, and experience.
8. Duty to follow due process.
9. Duty to foresee potentially harmful. circumstances and situations
10. Duty to plan.
11. Duty to keep records.
12. Duty to provide safe transportation.

Reprinted by permission, copyright 1989, Samuel H. Adams and *Athletic Business* Magazine.

Adams (1990, May) cites legal duties in Exhibit 7–1. Adhering to these guidelines would not only minimize injuries or loss but would indicate that the personnel were acting within a standard of care as prudent individuals. Further, any individual selected to instruct or supervise participants must be qualified to do so. Responsible administrators select staff whose qualities and credentials equip them for the delineated tasks within their expected roles.

[Bishop v. Fair Lanes Georgia Bowling, Inc., 803 Federal Reporter, 2d. U.S. Court of Appeals, 11th Circuit, 1548, November 12, 1986]

Facts: Several patrons were assaulted by other patrons in the parking lot outside of the bowling alley. On a Saturday morning around 2:00 A.M., two groups of loud drunks came out of the bowling alley. Words were exchanged by the two groups and a fight ensued. One of the groups brought charges against the proprietor, claiming that he should have been able to foresee the potential for violence.

Issues: Could the proprietor foresee the potential of a conflict, and therefore be negligent? Did the proprietor of the bowling alley fail to exercise ordinary care in keeping his premises safe?

Decision: The court ruled against the bowling alley because the bowling alley kept serving the defendants beer after they had obviously been drinking too much. The court also ruled against the bowling alley because they found the bowling alley failed to protect the plaintiff from apparent and foreseeable dangers. The precedent case was Donaldson v. Olympic Spa, 333 S.E. (2) 98.

[Vines v. Birmingham Baseball Club, 450 Southern Edition, 2d. Supreme Court of Alabama, 455, May 11, 1984]

Facts: On August 6, 1982, appellant Vines attended a professional baseball game at Birmingham's Rickwood Field in the company of his wife and another couple. He bought a ticket to the game, and sat beyond the seated areas protected by screens. During the game Vines was struck in the face by a baseball that was batted by a Birmingham Baron. He suffered serious facial injuries. Vines filed the action alleging that the Birmingham Baseball Club was negligent because they breached their duty as operator of the field by failing to warn them specifically of the potential hazards inherent to the sport of baseball.

Issue: Did Vines assume the risk when he bought the ticket to the game? Was the baseball club negligent? Were there warning signs of potential danger placed where they could easily be seen?

Decision: The court ruled in favor of the baseball club. The court said that the plaintiff was sufficiently warned of the dangers. Some key cases used in the case were Anderson v. Kansas City Baseball Club, 231 S.W. (2) 170, Keys v.

Alamo City Baseball Company, 150 S.W. (2) 368, and Edling v. Kansas City Baseball & Exhibition, 168 S.W. 908.

Standard of care within risk management programs also applies to facilities, the weight room, aquatics, intramural activities and all equipment (Brzycki, 1988, January; Dougherty, 1985, August). Of further importance is the fact that some insurance companies are willing to reduce costs of insurance if the agency demonstrates it is using a sound risk management prevention program ("A pay-off," 1987, March; "Risk management," June).

PROTECTIVE EQUIPMENT—REGULATIONS, CHANGES, AND SUGGESTIONS

Many of the country's national associations, sporting goods manufacturers, and some insurance companies are advocating continued research to make sporting, recreational, and fitness equipment as safe as can reasonably be expected. The National Operating Committee on Standards for Athletic Equipment (NOCSAE), National Collegiate Athletic Association (NCAA), National Federation of State High School Associations (NFSHSA), National Youth Sports Coaches Association (NYSCA), National Athletic Training Association (NATA), National Strength and Conditioning Association (NSCA), American Coaching Effectiveness Program (ACEP), Rawlings, Worth, Athletic Technology Inc. (ATI), Kenko, Wilson, and Riddell, to name several, continue to monitor, suggest, and initiate standards and regulations to provide safer protective equipment for athletic/recreational enthusiasts.

One group, previously mentioned, the Athletic Equipment Managers Association (AEMA), has instituted a certification program to improve the knowledge and promote education of athletic equipment managers ("Equipment managers," 1990, October 22).

As mentioned by Dr. Marlene Adrian (1990, Summer), several certification bodies for various sports evaluate the specifications of protective equipment, materials, and playing surfaces. Some of the councils are: the Hockey Equipment Certification Council (HECC), Eye Safety Certification Council (ESCC), NOCSAE, the Football Sports Equipment and Facilities Committee of the American Society for Testing Materials (ASTM), and the Consumer Products Safety Commission.

Dr. Adrian (op. cit., p. 11) suggests five guidelines for protective equipment: "(1) It must be selected with respect to the injuries and probable trauma sites, as defined by the sport; (2) It must fit the athlete properly; (3) It must conform to standards, to certification, or, if such guidelines do not exist, to scientific criteria; (4) The types worn must be continually evaluated; (5) Its use must include an educational process." Athletes and other enthusiasts must know how to use, wear, and fit the equipment properly.

Coaches and other practitioners must inform the participants of the regulations and standards set forth in the manufacturer's warning and product label. Many interested professionals have reported on the personal care, use, protection, fit, and liability of various protective equipment. Specific regulations and safety factors associated with protective equipment are discussed in more detail by Burke (1988, January), Easterbrook (1987, June), Haines (1987, March), McCarthy (1988, December), Olson (1981, September), Boss (cited in "Back to basics," 1989, March), and Watkins (1989, January and 1990, January)

Innovative changes appearing on the market include, but are not limited to, the following products: a softer, safer baseball/softball for youth sports participants ("Safer balls," 1990, November) and ("Worth RIF," 1990, January); breakaway/ releasable bases for baseball/softball (Loosli et al., 1988, July), ("Sliding in," 1989, July), (Dahlberg, 1989, March 1); and an air football helmet system ("Air football," 1990, January), (The evaluation, 1987, November). Innovative equipment changes are occurring in other sports and activities, such as bicycling, skiing, ice hockey, racket sports, volleyball, and soccer. There are new designs for knee braces, hip-, shoulder-, and kneepads, safety goggles and eye glasses, volleyballs and soccer balls. Also, graphite and ceramic bats are being researched and various lengths and types of skis are being produced for the beginner and advanced slope enthusiast. There continues to be a search for the ever better protective equipment in an attempt to make sports and activities safer for participants and, in the process, reduce costly litigation.

Exhibit 7–2 shows the methods that Stotlar (1987, January, p. 29) presents to reduce the possibility of injury or loss as well as lessen the chance for lawsuits.

Exhibit 7–2 ■ Suggestions for Selection and Use of Protective Equipment

1. Purchase athletic equipment from reputable manufacturers.
2. Purchase the safest equipment that resources will allow.
3. Be sure that the person who assembles the equipment is competent to do so and follows all manufacturer's instructions.
4. Adequately maintain all pieces of athletic equipment according to the manufacturer's guidelines.
5. Use equipment only for the purpose for which it was designed.
6. Warn all participants of all possible risks entailed in using the equipment.
7. Avoid using homemade equipment.
8. Do not allow participants to use defective equipment.

Exhibit reprinted with permission from JOPERD (Journal of Physical Education, Recreation, and Dance), January 1987, pp. 27–29. JOHPERD is a publication of the American Alliance for Health, Physical Education, Recreation and Dance, 1900 Association Drive, Reston, VA 22091–1599.

EXHIBIT 7-3 ■ **Preventative Management Techniques**

1. Provide for proper, adequate, and qualified supervision. Know CPR, first aid, and so forth.
2. Know the working details of all your equipment and place warning and use/misuse labels in visible places along the equipment. Users must be able to view the signs as they normally approach the workout area or equipment.
3. Check and maintain the equipment/facilities on a regular basis. Document the results.
4. Position the equipment in patterns and to allow better traffic flow and prevent members from accidentally bumping into weight racks, each other, and so on.
5. Place appropriate equipment in proper use areas or rooms.
6. Remove/replace hazardous, broken equipment.
7. Continue to provide a safe environment.
8. Instruct those who need it. Education is a part of the total package.

Adapted from Samuel H. Adams, "Legal Duties of Coaches," *Athletic Business,* March 1989, pp. 32, 34, 37, and "Prevention Pays in Club Safety," September 1987, pp. 44, 46–47. Reprinted by permission, copyright 1989, Samuel H. Adams and *Athletic Business* Magazine.

HEALTH AND FITNESS CLUBS—WARNINGS AND SUGGESTIONS

Part of the challenge faced by health and fitness spa owners is that not only do they have to concern themselves with the facilities and equipment, but they must also train and supervise their fitness instructors, maintenance employees, visitors and members of the club (Rabinoff, 1989) to be aware of legal responsibilities. Lawsuits and major problems have been reported in the following main areas: saunas, steam rooms, and hot tubs (Stamford, 1989, May); weight rooms; aerobic spaces; exercise and sports areas; and improper, inadequate and unqualified supervision (Kerr and Ryan, 1988, April), ("Fitness kick," 1989, January), ("Accident-proofing," 1988, July), (Freeman, 1989, vol. 11, No. 2), and ("Prevention pays," 1987, September). Risk management experts provide suggestions and preventative management techniques that may lessen the probability of a court case, as well as possibly reduce the costs of liability insurance. Exhibit 7–3 includes some of their suggestions. Incorporating the suggestions into facility operations should establish a sound plan for risk management—a plan to stop problems before they occur. The following serves as an example.

[Tucker v. Trotter Treadmills, 779 P. 2d, Supreme Court of Montana, 524, September 19, 1989]

Facts: The plaintiff club patron filed suit against a treadmill manufacturer contending that it failed to properly instruct patrons as to the use of its equipment. The club patron contended that the treadmill was defective because it was not equipped with a safety device which would prevent it from starting at a high rate of speed. On April 9, 1984, the patron went to the club, "the Courthouse," to exercise. At some point during her workout, she decided to use one of the motorized exercise treadmills, which she had not used before. While stepping on the treadmill and turning on the machine, the belt began to move and the plaintiff immediately fell, injuring her shoulder. She had received instruction on how to use the facility's equipment in 1978, but when she rejoined the club, she neither requested nor received any more instruction. She thought she could operate it, however, because she had seen others using it.

Issue: Although no warnings or instructions were displayed on the treadmill, there were three posters of instructions and warnings on the wall directly behind the motorized treadmill. The court found that these instructions and warnings would have been "clearly visible" to anyone approaching the device. The plaintiff indicated, however, that she did not notice the posted instructions or warnings and, therefore, did not read them.

Decision: The Montana Supreme Court found that the trial court had appropriately granted summary judgment to the defendant. The court found that no evidence was presented to indicate that the warnings and instructions were anything other than proper.

Despite the seemingly difficult obstacles to hurdle and potential lawsuits to avoid, Dr. Marlene Adrian (1990, May, pp. 16–17) indicates a bright future for health and fitness spas because "fitness equipment in the future will better respond to the needs of each athlete [and club member] and therefore will be much safer for all users." Improvements, Adrian continues, will be in "safety designs, safety education, developing standards, and enhanced technology."

LIABILITY INSURANCE

It is evident that product liability, injury-related lawsuits, and huge jury awards have driven the costs of liability insurance to an astonishing level.

Lubell (1987, September) reports that lacrosse equipment maker, William H. Brine, paid $8,000 a year for $25 million of insurance. Then in 1985 he was notified that the cost would be $200,000 per $1 million of protection. He decided to go uninsured and, reportedly, he is not alone. Jacki (1989, May–June) relates that because of skyrocketing insurance costs and heavy injury awards, Nissen, the gymnastics equipment giant, was forced to shut down. The same has been documented for approximately 18 of the original 20 helmet manufacturers. Tolls have been taken in sports, but much is being done to improve the situation.

Richard Feldman (cited in Goulian, 1988, July 25, p. 45), "an attorney and champion of product liability reform legislation," reports that insurers may agree that a product is safer in reality. However, they don't care about reality, they care about what may be proven in court. The problem for some still remains: "the inability of the entrepreneur to get liability insurance" (Goulian, 1988, July 25, p. 41). Fortunately, there are some insurance companies willing to reduce liability insurance costs if the agency has in operation and on file a sound, viable risk management plan. It would be wise for each facility to develop and adhere to a risk management policy for all employees.

One policy helpful in reducing liability is an "Agreement to Participate" (refer to Legal Terms section for a strong consent form), or informed consent (Lubell, 1987, September). It is also recommended that coaches, fitness and wellness managers, sports administrators, and the like, meet with parents/guardians and participants to explain in detail the inherent risks in the sport or activity. A discussion on the possibility of injury and/or death must be included. When all factors have been reported to the individuals, a detailed consent form must be signed by the parent/guardian and by the participant before engaging in the event or sport.

Simply stated, because of a suit-sensitive society and large court awards to injured parties, all this is necessary for the survival of sports, recreational pursuits, and protection of the agency and its employees or volunteers. Managers must become detail-oriented, acquire knowledge of the law, institute a written management plan, and purchase comprehensive liability insurance from a reputable professional organization.

GENERAL SAFETY FACTORS—A SELF-HELP PROCESS

Thygerson (1986, p. 56) offers an encouraging thought in that, "We should not live by a timid and faint-hearted value. Safety is a positive concept, not a negative one. It is not meant to be a 'thou-shalt-not' approach to life that holds people back."

It is obvious that what one person considers a risk, another does not. There are persons who "throw caution to the wind" in almost every situation, and there are those who demonstrate an overly protective or cautious approach to life. Both styles can be a hazard to the health and general well-being of that individual as well as others.

[Scott vs. State, 158 New York Supplement 2d. Court of Claims New York, 617, November 30, 1956]

Facts: In the spring of 1956 two baseball teams were playing a conference game. Scott played center field for his team. Inside of the fence in center field was a flagpole. A ball was hit to center field. While running back to catch the ball, Scott ran into the flagpole and Scott suffered injuries due to the collision.

Issues: Was the school district negligent in its duties because it had not properly maintained the playing field? Did Scott assume the risk of being injured by being on the team?

Decision: The court found in favor of the plaintiff, because the school district was negligent since it was their duty to maintain and keep the field as safe as possible. The court said that Scott did not assume the risk of injury by participating on the team, and awarded him $12,000 in damages.

In another case, the Kentucky Court of Appeals ruled that the negligence of a coach in wiring a homemade whirlpool bath caused the electrocution of a young athlete in Bourbon County.

[Massie v. Persson, 729 S.W. 2d. Court of Appeals Kentucky, 448, March 6, 1987]

Facts: Ronald Gregory Massie died in the whirlpool at Bourbon County Junior High School after a school baseball game on April 17, 1980. His mother, Patricia Massie, filed a wrongful-death suit against Persson, who was the school's football coach, and against five contractors involved in building the school in the late 1960s.

Issues: An electrical outlet that figured in the death was not properly grounded, but the judges agreed with the trial court that the contractors were exempted by a five-year statute of limitations. The appellate opinion described how Persson, who wanted a whirlpool larger than the school's one-man stainless-steel model, built a concrete block pool and rigged it with an agitator and with controls he had taken from the other unit. The controls were held in place with athletic tape, and the power cord and plug also were held together with tape.

Decision: The appeals court said there would have been no accident if Persson had installed a "ground fault interrupter" on his device, as required by the 1975 National Electric Code.

A blend of reasonableness, prudence, and risk-taking, certainly pertain to the worksite and lifestyle of coaches, sports and recreational administrators, health and fitness managers, principals, entrepreneurs, and others in similar positions. The basic suggestions mentioned in risk management plans, protective equipment standards, warnings and regulations, and adherence to the rules of the game aptly apply to safety factors.

Obremsky (1977, January) suggests that school personnel must evaluate the fitness of athletes as well as the equipment used on a regular and documented basis. Staruf (1990, July) recommends that personnel develop a sound purchasing plan and ask specific, meaningful questions to determine if the equipment is exactly what is needed for the program and to ascertain the manufacturer's return policy on unwanted items. This must be planned prior to purchasing items. He further notes that, for obvious reasons, concerns for purchasing wearing apparel differ from concerns associated with the purchase of protective equipment.

A careful and regular inspection of helmets coupled with a knowledge of reconditioning standards and procedures specified by the manufacturer, as well as NOCSAE, is suggested by Kelly (1989, May). He further implies that such action will help insure the safety of the program's athletes. Baron (1990, May, p. 21) states that the claim of 'failure to warn' has become one of the most prevalent allegations in sports injury lawsuits today."

Baron (1990, May, p. 22) suggests an orientation meeting after which parents and participants sign an "informed consent" or an Agreement to Participate form. An individual with a pre-existing injury should never be involved in an activity or sport unless and until a release is granted by an attending physician. If the injury might be aggravated through participation, a detailed post-injury consent form should be signed by the athlete. "By signing this consent form, the student-athlete assumes the risk of sustaining a more serious injury rather than the athletic department."

Cherry, et al. (1990, May) present the detailed procedures utilized by the University of Washington's football program. The in-depth risk management plan should use specified consent forms, include medical history, and apply restrictions when a medical condition is discovered. The plan is designed to reduce the athletic department's liability, to inform the athlete of inherent risks, and about their responsibilities for their own health and safety. It becomes prudent for sports, fitness, or recreation managers to adopt the practice of attaching manufacturer's warning labels to a form for the participants and/or the parents/guardians to sign.

Safety checklists are available for a variety of settings including, but not limited to: outdoor programs (Olson, 1985, December), playground equipment ("National survey," 1988, September), exercise facilities and equipment (Herbert & Herbert, 1988, February), recreational/sport/exercise programs (Clement, 1988, Spring), profile, evaluation, and assessment of legal aspects in sport (Penman & Adams, 1980), and general safety factors (Borkowski, 1987, November/December).

A final safety factor is the need for qualified or certified practitioners. Martens (1988, October) states that certification of coaches is necessary to lessen litigation and should be attained through training programs and accredited curriculums. In the NCAA News ("Equipment managers," 1990, October 22) it was reported that the Athletic Equipment Managers Association (AEMA) will begin a certification process for its members. To retain active certification in the AEMA, equipment managers will have to complete continuing-education programs. (More information is available from AEMA, 723 Keil Court, Bowling Green, Ohio 43402, telephone 419/352–1207.)

SUMMARY

The United States Constitution is the ultimate authority for establishing sovereign power in the United States (Edginton & Williams, 1978). This fact, coupled with a suit-sensitive society, presents interesting courtroom situations for determining negligence and making awards to the wronged parties.

This chapter presents information relative to general liability factors; product liability considerations; the necessity for risk management procedures; warnings and regulations associated with protective equipment; practical suggestions and cautions for health and fitness clubs/spas relative to equipment and facility safety; trends applying to liability insurance, the skyrocketing costs and the difficulty of obtaining insurance due to legal liability occurrences; and general safety factors with emphasis on a self-help process.

Primary emphasis is on providing a sound, documented risk management program, which is beneficial in litigation matters, and may reduce insurance costs because some insurance companies have begun to lower rates for agencies wih risk management policies.

Educating personnel and parents/guardians and/or the participants about the inherent risks of sports and activities, and signing "informed consent' forms, are major steps in the sharing of legal responsibilities. Everyone involved with dangerous activities must be aware of product liability laws, warning labels, and the "foreseeability" factor associated with products and facilities. Through qualified personnel and precise risk management plans, it is possible to reduce risk, injury, and the probability of major litigation.

SELECTED READINGS

Accident-proofing your weight room. (1988, July). *Athletic Business,* pp. 52–55.

Adams, S. (1989, March). Legal duties of coaches. *Athletic Business,* pp. 32–37.

Adrian, M. (1990, May). Fitness in the future. *College Athletic Magazine,* pp. 16–17.

Adrian, M. (1990, Summer). Covering the risk. *Training and Conditioning,* pp. 11–13.

Air football helmet system provides better player comfort. *Athletic Business,* pp. 66–67.

A payoff for prevention? (1987, March). .*Athletic Business,* pp. 36–40.

Appenzeller, H., & Appenzeller, T. (1980). *Sports and the courts,* pp. 113–117. Charlottesville, VA: Michie.

Back to basics on fitting helmets. (1989, March). *Athletic Business,* pp. 38–41.

Baley, J. A., & Matthews D. L. (1989). *Law and liability in athletics, physical education, and recreation.* (2d ed.). Dubuque, IA: Wm. C. Brown.

Baron, R. (1988, September). Risk management, the defensive game plan. *Parks & Recreation,* pp. 53–55.

Baron, R. (1990, May). The attorney's perspective. *College Athletic Magazine,* pp. 21–22.

Borkowski, R. (1987, December). How to avoid athletic law suits. *The First Aider,* p. 5.

Brzycki, M. (1988, January). Coaches responsible for weight room safety. *Athletic Business,* pp. 30–36.

Bucher, C. A. (1987). *Management of physical education and athletic programs,* pp. 340–371. (9th ed.). St. Louis, MO: Times Mirror/Mosby.

Burke, E. (1988, January). Safety standards for bicycle helmets. *The Physician and Sports Medicine,* pp. 148–153.

The challenges facing organized sports programs in the U.S. today. (1980, April). *Athletic Purchasing and Facilities,* pp. 10–14.

Cherry, E., et al. (1990, May). Insuring protection. *College Athletic Magazine,* pp. 18, 20–21.

Clement, A. (1988, Spring). A selected checklist of risk management in recreational sport exercise programs. *IAHPERD Journal,* pp. 18–20.

Dahlberg, T. (1989, March 1). Inventor claims breakaway bases will reduce injuries sharply. *NCAA News,* p. 6.

Dougherty, N. (1985, August). Intramural liability, check out these checklists for safety precautions in intramural facilities, equipment, supervision, and participant instruction. *Journal of Physical Education, Recreation, and Dance,* pp. 45–49.

Easterbrook, M. (1987, June). Eye protection in racket sports: An update. *The Physician and Sports Medicine,* pp. 180–192.

Edginton, C. R., & Williams, J. G. (1978). *Productive management of leisure service organizations,* pp. 356–370. New York: John Wiley.

Equipment managers can be certified. (1990, October 22). *NCAA News,* p. 16.

The evaluation of protective equipment. (1987, November). *Athletic Business,* pp. 47–49.

Fitness kick may lead to pain for hoteliers. (1989, January). *Hospitality Law,* pp. 1–2.

Freeman, J. (1988). Guidelines for safe and effective strength program administration. NSCA Journal), pp. 44, 46–47.

Frost, R. B., Lockhart, B. D., & Marshall, S. J. (1988). *Administration of physical education and athletics,* pp. 381–403. (3rd ed.). Dubuque, IA: Wm. C. Brown.

Goulian, L. (1988, July 25). Sports wares, the murder of invention. *Sports Inc.,* pp. 44–45.

Grace, P. (1989, March). Risky business, risk management involves asking the right questions before the accident happens. *College Athletic Magazine,* pp. 20–23.

Haines, A. (1987, March). Fit your football equipment for safety and comfort. *Scholastic Coach,* pp. 38–49, 70–72.

Herbert, D. & Herbert, W. (1988, February). Frequent claims and suits in equipment-related injuries. *Fitness Management,* p. 22.

Horine, L. (1991). *Administration of physical education and sport programs,* pp. 89–114. (2nd ed.). Dubuque, IA: Wm. C. Brown.

Jacki, M. (1989, May–June). Nissen forced to close, a lesson must be learned. *USA Gymnastics,* p. 4.

Jefferies, S. C. (1985). *Sport law study guide. American Coaching Effectiveness Programs.* Champaign, IL: Human Kinetics.

Kaiser, R. A. (1986). *Liability & law in recreation, parks, and sports.* Englewood Cliffs, NJ: Prentice Hall.

Kelly, B. (1989, May). Heads up. *College Athletic Magazine,* pp. 28–30.

Kerr, B., & Ryan, H. (1988, April). $84,500 verdict against ¡44 ¡health club for failure to train plaintiff on use of squat machine. *Trial Talk,* p. 123.

Kraus, R. G., & Curtis, J. E. (1982). *Creative management in recreation and parks,* pp. 298–302. (3rd ed.). St. Louis, MO: Mosby.

Loosli, et al. (1988, July). Injuries in slow-pitch softball, *The Physician and Sports Medicine,* pp. 110–118.

Lubell, A. (1987, September). Insurance, liability, and the American way of sport. *The Physician and Sports Medicine,* pp. 192–200.

Martens, R. (1988, October). Coaching. *Athletic Business,* pp. 22–24.

McCarthy, P. (1988, December). Prophylactic knee braces: Where do they stand? *The Physician and Sports Medicine,* pp. 102–110, 115.

National survey identifies areas of concern for playground equipment. (1988, September). *AAHPERD Update.*

Obrensky, P. (1977, January). School must check fitness of its athletes, equipment. *The First Aider,* pp. 3, 14–15.

Olson, J. (1981, September). Safety standards for athletic and physical education facilities, equipment, and practices. *Athletic Purchasing and Facilities,* pp. 48–52.

Olson J. (1985, December). Safety checklists: how safe are your outdoor programs? *Athletic Business,* pp. 48–50.

Penman, K. & Adams, S. (1980). *Assessing athletic and physical education programs.* Dubuque, IA: Wm. C. Brown.

Prevention pays in club safety. (1987, September). *Athletic Business,* pp. 44, 46–47.

Product liability reform, will new political winds change the course? (1987 January). *Athletic Business,* pp. 36–38.

Rabinoff, M. (1989, a presentation). Risk management and the safety audit: Its use and importance for health and fitness clubs/centers. *Rabinoff Consulting Services,* Littleton, CO.

Raybon, P. (1984, December 3). Caveat, sports consultant blasts fitness-instruction quality. *Rocky Mountain News.* Denver, CO., p. 43.

Risk management is the best insurance. (1987, June). *Athletic Business,* pp. 36–40.

Safer balls for kids. (1990, November). *Athletic Business,* pp. 10, 13.

Seefeldt, V. (Ed.). (1987). *Handbook for youth sports coaches,* p. 5. National Association of Sport and Physical Education, Reston, VA: AAHPERD.

Sliding in safely. (1989, July). *Athletic Business,* pp. 11–13.

Stamford, B. (1989, May). Saunas, steam rooms, and hot tubs. *The Physician and Sports Medicine,* p. 188.

Staruf, D. (1990, July). Minding your q's. *College Athletic Magazine,* pp. 18–19.

Stotlar, D. (1987, January). Athletic equipment, product liability gone awry. *Journal of Physical Education, Recreation, and Dance,* pp. 27–29.

Swartz, E. (1989, August). When products injure children. *Trial,* pp. 50–54.

Thygerson, A. L. (1986). *Safety,* pp. 39–49, 50–56, 91–93, 284. (2nd ed.). Englewood Cliffs, NJ: Prentice Hall.

Watkins, S. (1989, January). Padding against injury. *College Athletic Magazine,* pp. 25–27.

Watkins, S. (1990, January). Shouldering the blow. *College Athletic Magazine,* pp. 30–32.

Wong, G. (1988). *Essentials of amateur sports law.* Dover, MA: Auburn House.

Worth RIF baseballs, softballs first to receive NOCSAE stamp. (1990, January). *Athletic Business,* p. 66.

Appendix A

SPORTS AND RECREATION FOR THE DISABLED: OPPORTUNITIES, EQUIPMENT, AND RESOURCES

Carol Mushett, Health, Physical Education, and Recreation, Wayne State University

More than 46 million Americans have a significant disability. Approximately 75 percent of these are between the ages of 16 and 64. More than 15% of the population in the United States is disabled. More than 40% of the general population has an immediate family member with a disability and close to 90% of the population has an extended family member with a disability (Wyeth, p. 5).

Historically, relatively few persons with disabilities have actively pursued the full range of sports and recreation opportunities open to nondisabled individuals. This has clearly changed, however, due to the passage and implementation of Public Law 94-142, which requires free and appropriate education for handicapped children in the least restrictive environment, and of Public Law 95-606, the Amateur Sports Act mandating that the United States Olympic Committee ensure competitive sports opportunities for athletes with disabilities (Sherrill, pp. 31, 43).

There is great progress. There are currently more than 200 national and local organizations devoted to the development and provision of sports and recreation opportunities for children and adults with handicapping characteristics. The most notable of these are the seven Disabled Sport Organizations (DSO), which are officially recognized by the United States Olympic Committee as the national governing bodies of sports for the disabled (Paciorek & Jones p. 24).

Each of these DSO's is a member of the United States Olympic Committee and serves as the United States Organizational representative in the appropriate international sports governing bodies (see Exhibit A–1). The combined participa

Exhibit A–1 ■ Group E Members of the United States Olympic Committee

American Athletic Association for the Deaf
    (AAD)
1134 Davenport Drive
Burton, MI 48529
(313) 239-3962

Dwarf Athletic Association of America
    (DAAA)
3725 West Holmes Road
Lansing, MI 48911
(517) 344-6133

National Handicapped Sports (NHS)
1145 19th Street, N.W., Suite 717
Washington, D.C. 20036
(301) 652-7505

National Wheelchair Athletic Association
    (NWAA)
1604 East Pikes Peak Avenue
Colorado Springs, CO 80909
(719) 635-9300

Special Olympics (SO)
1350 New York Avenue, N.W., Suite 500
Washington, D.C. 20005
(202) 628-3630

United States Association for Blind Athletes
    (USABA)
33 North Institute, Brown Hall, Suite 015
Colorado Springs, CO 80903
(719) 630-0422

United States Cerebral Palsy Athletic
    Association (USCPAA)
34518 Warren Road, Suite 264
Westland, MI 48185
(313) 425-8961

**Emerging Group *not*
a Group E Member**

U.S. Les Autres Sports Association
1101 Post Oak, Suite 9–486
Houston, TX 77056

---

tion of these seven organizations exceeds one million children and adults. The DSO's provide rule books, resource manuals, and technical assistance to people in local programs and facilities who wish to develop sports and recreation opportunities for the disabled.

On July 26, 1990, President George Bush signed into law the most far-reaching disability legislation to date. The Americans with Disabilities Act (ADA) is a comprehensive civil rights legislation that is clear, strong, and enforceable. The ADA will have a direct and widespread effect on the disabled consumer's access to recreation and sports opportunities. It also has direct implications on facilities, equipment, programs, and service providers.

This legislation applies to all businesses, programs, and agencies that have public access. Any recreation, sports/service provider is now required to provide "reasonable accommodation" to any consumer regardless of handicapping characteristic. This includes the provision of a barrier-free environment, but access to recreation and sports opportunities goes far beyond handicapped parking and ramps. Not only must facilities be accessible, but programs and services must also be usable. Disabled consumers can now expect and legally demand accommodations, including the provision of adaptive equipment, to enable their participation.

The ADA regulations are currently being formulated. It is reasonable to anticipate that facilities currently providing recreational participants with equipment, either separately or in concert with a facility fee, will begin to offer adaptive equipment to consumers with individual differences.

For example, a commercial ski slope that rents skis to customers may also rent outriggers, an adapted version of a forearm crutch and a miniski that provides additional balance for disabled 3-track skiers (one ski and two outriggers) (Paciorek & Jones, p. 248). Another common accommodation is the provision of ramps or chutes for bowlers with significant physical limitations.

Most programmatic accommodations do not require significant cost or undue burden, but many recreation and sport administrators need more information about the adaptive equipment available to them. Numerous books and catalogs address the many types of adaptive recreation equipment on the market. See the References for books that could prove invaluable in providing inclusive recreation opportunities for consumers with disabilities.

No longer will disabled children and adults be limited by the segregated programs of the past. Inclusive recreation that allows for individual differences is the moral and legal responsibility of all programs, facilities, and services for the public.

REFERENCES

Nesbitt, J. A. (1986). *The international directory of recreation-oriented assistive device sources.* Marina Del Rey, CA: Lifeboat Press.

Paciorek, M. J., & Jones, J. A. (1986). *Sports and recreation for the disabled: A resource manual.* Indianapolis, IN: Benchmark.

Sherrill, C. (1986). *Adapted physical education and recreation.* Dubuque, IA: Wm. C. Brown.

Wyeth, D. O. (1989). Breaking barriers and changing attitudes. *Journal of Osteopathic Medicine, 3*(4), 5–10.

Appendix B
COMPLIANCE WITH TITLE IX

For more information regarding Title IX of the Education Amendments of 1972, here are some resources:

Anyone's Guide to Filing a Title IX Complaint. Available from the Project on Equal Education Rights, 1333 H Street, NW, 11th Floor, Washington, DC 20005. Telephone: (202) 682-0940. ($1.25)

The Title IX Information Pack. Women's Sports Foundation, 342 Madison Avenue, Suite 728, New York, NY 10173. Telephone: (800) 227-3988 or (212) 972-9170 in New York. ($2.00)

Title IX: A practical guide to achieving sex equity in education. Write on the envelope: "Attention: Title IX: A Practical Guide," National Women's Law Center, 1616 P Street, NW, Washington, DC 20036. ($3.00)

DEPARTMENT OF EDUCATION OFFICE FOR CIVIL RIGHTS

HEADQUARTERS
Department of Education
Office for Civil Right
330 C Street, SW
Washington, DC 20202
(202) 732-1213

REGION I
Regional Director
Office for Civil Rights, Region I
Department of Education
J.W. McCormick Post Office and Courthouse,
    Room 222
Boston, MA 02109
(617) 223-9662

REGION II
Regional Director
Office for Civil Rights, Region II
Department of Education
26 Federal Plaza, 33rd Floor
New York, NY 10278
(212) 264-5180

REGION III
Regional Director
Office for Civil Rights, Region III
Department of Education
Gateway Building, Room 6300
3535 Market Street
Philadelphia, PA 19101
(215) 596-6787

REGION IV
Regional Director
Office for Civil Rights, Region IV
Department of Education
P.O. Box 1705
Atlanta, GA 30301
(404) 221-2954

REGION V
Regional Director
Office for Civil Rights, Region V
Department of Education
401 South State Street, 7th Floor
Chicago, IL 60605
(312) 886-3456

REGION VI
Regional Director
Office for Civil Rights, Region VI
Department of Education
Room 1935, 1200 Main Tower Building
Dallas, TX 75202
(214) 767-3959

REGION VII
Acting Regional Director
Office for Civil Rights, Region VII
Department of Education
10220 North Executive Hills Blvd.
P.O. Box 901381
Kansas City, MO 641901381

REGION VIII
Regional Director
Office for Civil Rights, Region VIII
Department of Education
Federal Office Building
1961 Stout Street, Room 1185
Denver, CO 80294
(303) 837-5695

REGION IX
Acting Regional Director
Office for Civil Rights, Region IX
Department of Education
221 Main Street, 10th Floor
San Francisco, CA 94103
(415) 227-8042

REGION X
Regional Director
Office for Civil Rights, Region X
Department of Education
915 Second Avenue
Seattle, WA 98174–1099
(206) 399-1635

Appendix C
SPORTS EQUIPMENT ASSOCIATIONS

Athletic Equipment Managers Association
723 Keil Court
Bowling Green, OH 43402
(419) 352-1207

Canadian Sporting Goods Association
4550, rue St-Antoine W., Suite 510
Montreal, Quebec, CN
H2Z 1j1
(514) 393-1132
Fax: (514) 393-9513

National Athletic Equipment
Reconditioners Association
Continental Athletics
P.O. Box 128
1050 Hazel Street
Gridley, CA 95948
(916) 846-4711

National Operating Committee on
Standards for Athletic Equipment
101 Matthei Building
Wayne State University
Detroit, MI 48202
(313) 577-4280

National School Supply and Equipment
Association
8300 Colesville Road
2nd Floor
Silver Spring, MD 20910
(703) 524-8819

National Sporting Goods Association
1699 Wall Street
Mt. Prospect, IL 60056
(708) 439-4000

Sporting Goods Manufacturers Association
200 Castlewood Drive
North Palm Beach, FL 33408
(407) 842-4100

Appendix D

COMPUTER SOFTWARE FOR SPORTS EQUIPMENT

Athletic Equipment Management System
J. Garner & Associates
2710 Mustang Drive, Suite 100
Herndon, Virginia 22071
(703) 689-3579

Cornell University's Software Program for Equipment Inventory
Equipment Manager
Schoellkoepf Equipment Room
Cornell University
Ithaca, NY 14850

Index